ALSO BY PACO UNDERHILL

Why We Buy: The Science of Shopping
Call of the Mall

The Global Marketplace Turns Female-Friendly

PACO UNDERHILL

WHAT WOMEN WANT

Simon & Schuster
New York London Toronto Sydney

Simon & Schuster
1230 Avenue of the Americas
New York, NY 10020

First Simon & Schuster hardcover edition July 2010

SIMON & SCHUSTER and colophon are registered trademarks of Simon & Schuster, Inc.

For information about special discounts for bulk purchases, please contact Simon & Schuster Special Sales at 1-866-506-1949 or business@simonandschuster.com.

The Simon & Schuster Speakers Bureau can bring authors to your live event. For more information or to book an event, contact the Simon & Schuster Speakers Bureau at 1-866-248-3049 or visit our website at www.simonspeakers.com.

Designed by Jill Putorti

Manufactured in the United States of America

10 9 8 7 6 5 4 3 2 1

Library of Congress Cataloging-in-Publication Data is available.

ISBN 978–1–4165–6995–4
ISBN 978–1–4165–7020–2 (ebook)

To Uncle Toby and Aunt Aubrey, with gratitude and love

CONTENTS

INTRODUCTION

As I make my way around the world, I see it everywhere: the expanded cultural, social, and economic influence of women.

For a bald, aging retail wonk who's spent a lifetime wrestling with a stutter, and who Malcolm Gladwell described in his *New Yorker* magazine profile as "almost goofy looking," I do a lot of public speaking—at conventions, company meetings, retreats, and gala dinners. It comes to around forty paid engagements a year. They're good ways to drum up business and get some media attention. In just about every speech I deliver, I include one line:

"We live in a world that is owned by men, designed by men, and managed by men—and yet we expect women to be active participants in it."

People laugh. There's a lot of nodding. Men and women can both identify. From Singapore to Texas, from Dubai to Mexico City, from Dublin to São Paolo, one of the seminal questions I ask is, *What makes this package, product, space, design, or service "female-friendly"?*

I'm not trying to be provocative or condescending. I'm not bringing any moral or feminist agendas to the question, either.

I'm simply acknowledging the increased social and professional dominance of females across the world. It's a rapidly spreading evolution I am well positioned to observe, process, and describe within the physical world and the global marketplace, whether it can be seen physically, in packaging, cars, appliances, and clothing; places, such as homes, hotels, offices, stores, restaurants, and attractions; or in plain old everyday services, such as Internet commerce, maid services, banks, and rental car agencies.

Maybe you're already aware of the effect females have had on our culture. Maybe you simply had your suspicions. But the cumulative effect is striking, and in many cases dramatic.

For example, did you know that:

Approximately 70 percent of all American females work outside the home.

Women control not just a percentage of active income in the world—i.e., money they take home from their own jobs—but a large percentage of passive income, meaning family money, or money they've inherited.

Women dominate higher education. Most college and university campuses across the United States and Canada are 60-40 female.

Today, record numbers of females are studying engineering, physics, computer science, biology, and clinical psychology.

The top tiers of business—as well as of medicine, law, and science—are increasingly female, a trend that began in the 1970s, as women began to overrun educational programs that trained them to become lawyers, physicians, and architects—just a handful of professions that were once typically male.

With the exception of the pickup truck, females influence almost every successful car that's come out of Detroit, whether it's the family minivan or the half-tank, half-observation post, secure colossus known as the SUV (which was never intended to be a macho vehicle).

Women run households and companies, are attending business schools in record numbers, and make up an increasing percentage of today's global business travelers.

Females make up a huge majority of all book buyers in the United States.

Women are the acquisitioners of food on behalf of their entire families. They are behind farmers' markets and the organic food movement.

Women choreograph the social lives of their families, and have a decisive say as to whether or not the family will spend school break camping in Big Bend, sunbathing on Nantucket, or staying home.

Women continue to create their own films and TV shows, as well as their own brands of humor, visual art, and music.

Sure, some of these examples are more conspicuous than others. Some are downright stealthy—the way the organic food movement has taken off, for example, or the way that, despite current pay inequities across the entertainment industry, a wicked-witted female writer and comedian named Tina Fey completely skewed our last presidential election.

It will never be absolutely equal between the sexes, but women are catching up. And it's only going to get more noticeable.

Enough so that if you're a man running a business, and if the power and influence females wield hasn't completely registered on your radar screen, well, then, what you've got here is a failure to communicate. If your store, restaurant, bank, hotel lobby, mall, or other public space or amenity doesn't acknowledge the female factor, if it doesn't invite women in and make them feel at home, at ease, safe, hygienic, respected, and in control, if it doesn't take into account what women want and expect (which is a whole lot different from what men want and expect), well, then, it's bad business. You also risk losing forever a powerful majority of consumers who are more than happy—gleeful, even!—to tell all their friends and acquaintances about your dirty dressing rooms, subpar lighting, creepy hotel lobby, brusque customer service, dingy mirrors or no mirrors at all, and an overall vibe of being treated like a second-class citizen.

In my experience, women are pretty good at spreading the word.

* * *

In 2005, a magical statistic stood out: for the first time in history, young women under the age of thirty in the largest American cities overtook men in earning power.

It was a shift that began in the late 1990s in urban areas like Los Angeles and Dallas. By the year 2000, it had migrated to New York City, when male and female wages came in more or less at a dead heat. Five years later, full-time working females between the ages of twenty-one and thirty living in one of the five boroughs of New York City brought home 117 percent of the wages of equivalent working males. To put it another way, for every guy pulling in a median salary of $30,560, an equivalent female was banking $35,653. And Texas isn't associated with big bucks, big hair, and big everything for nothing. In Dallas, women's wage-earning advantage over men was 120 percent—the highest in the nation.

Pay inequities between men and women? Everyone knows they're still out there. But in early 2009, President Obama signed an equal-pay bill designed to end gender-based income disparities. It's way overdue.

This increase in female earning power parallels employment figures around the globe. Starting in the United States, with its then-current 2009 employment rate of 8.5 percent, the chances of being twenty-five years old and gainfully employed are higher if you're a female than if you're a male. These odds go up even further if we don't consider immigrant, African-American, and Latino populations. Economic hard times favor females, too. During the recent recession, 82 percent of job losses befell men, who tend to be disproportionately represented in industries like construction and manufacturing. Historically, women are apt to work in fields such as education and health care, which are more resistant to economic swings.

One of the things I find fascinating about traveling overseas is observing how gender differences show up in various countries. In

Brazil, as in the United States, the unemployment rates for men are much higher than they are for women. In the Philippines, lower-class females can find work as domestics and childcare workers around the world, while the undereducated Filipino male has been completely marginalized.

Here's an obvious fact: The more highly educated you are, the better chance you have of being successfully employed in a well-paying job. Male or female, if you didn't manage to make it through high school, your unemployment rate hovers around 73 percent. A high school diploma raises your chance for some kind of employment by nearly 5 percent, but with a college or grad school degree, your professional opportunities go through the roof.

This could be one reason why women are pulling so far ahead in colleges and graduate schools. Currently 140 women are awarded bachelor degrees for every 100 men in the United States. It's a gender gap that's only expected to increase. Between 1969 and 2000, the number of male undergraduates increased by only 39 percent. At the same time, the number of female undergraduates rose by 157 percent. Females today are outpacing males in practically all post-secondary institutions, and also within African-American communities, where, according to one study, two university-educated women exist for every university-educated man.

Part of it can be attributed to the learning disabilities that are epidemic among young males. As of the early part of the twenty-first century, boys are nearly two and a half times more at risk than girls to suffer from reading disabilities. Dyslexia and autism spectrum disorders? Ten percent for boys as opposed to 6 percent for girls. In the United States, boys are also three times more likely than girls to be referred to a special education class, and twice as likely to have to repeat a school year (granted, sociodemographic factors, including the age of the parents and their own educational levels, can rearrange these statistics).

Then there's ADHD, short for attention deficit hyperactivity disorder. It covers a broad spectrum of diagnostic symptoms, ranging from inattentiveness to poor impulse control to restlessness and distractibility. Who gets it? Boys, mostly. It's just a fact. No one seems to know why, though there are a lot of theories bouncing around. Some educators believe that the norm for classroom behavior in grades K through 6—*shhhh . . . concentrate . . . focus . . .* —jives perfectly with the average young female temperament. Most little girls are comfortable sitting; little boys tend to squirm, fidget, and daydream. Whether we're talking about hyperactivity or dyslexia, often young boys aren't in their natural groove in the classroom while their female classmates thrive, which may ultimately help explain why females are making such educational giant steps.

Another critical reason women are making such headway in their careers—and really, I can't emphasize this enough—is babies. Or rather, the lack of them. Or rather, the option to choose if, when, and with whom you have one. We've stepped over a magical line in the history of our own human species. Thanks to birth control, we've decoupled sex from procreation and moved away from biology. Female sexuality, the reproductive kind, is in flux and in play. If you harbor any doubts, rent an old season or two of *Sex and the City*, or watch the movie. After graduating college or getting an advanced degree, many young women are in no hurry to pair up and settle down, which gives them the time, space, momentum, and luxury to pursue a professional track and make good money at it, too, at least in major American cities, where the social pressures to settle down and procreate aren't as great as they are in smaller or more rural areas of the country.

The ability to control the reproductive aspect of our lives has fundamentally changed some of the premises rooted in human beings as far back as the caves of eastern Africa. In my opinion, this isn't good or bad—it just is.

It has also transformed our world as we know it.

Muscle is something men have always brought to the table. But with the exception of, say, Scottish caber tossing, many industries that have historically required brute force—including farming and the military—no longer list "muscle" as part of the job description. In an increasingly digitalized world, the issue of massive biceps and triceps is becoming less relevant. Which comes as welcome news to the ninety-seven-pound weakling trying to defend his girl on the beach, and to women who can now very capably handle work that once called for male brawn.

Take the military. The present-day aircraft fighter? Chances are good the pilot of the new U.S. Air Force Predator is female. This long-endurance, medium-altitude, remotely piloted aircraft system is used for airborne surveillance and armed reconnaissance missions against critical targets. Imagery can be relayed in real time to a frontline soldier. The crew includes a pilot and a pair of sensor operators. Thanks to a hypersophisticated data link, they can fly the aircraft from inside a ground control station. The Predator is equipped with radar, infrared cameras, and two laser-guided AGM-114 Hellfire antiarmor missiles. No bulging biceps needed here—just smarts, focus, diligence, responsiveness, and pinpoint accuracy. Did anyone say "female"?

The woman as wage earner is a relatively recent concept, too. Though women have always worked, the evolution of the female economic powerhouse—the one who can spend money on whatever stuff *she* wants—is revolutionary, and growing fast. If women decide not to have children, it frees up income to be spent in other ways.

Another aspect of female economic power isn't active income but passive income. Active income refers to the female executive or employee who earns her own salary. Passive income can refer either to an inheritance, or to the spoils of what her hedge-funder husband left to his widow at age sixty-four when, after a career of seventy-hour weeks, he collapsed of a heart attack on the squash court. Both in the United States and in Japan, a significant amount of passive wealth is held in the hands of women. They're spending it, too. They're taking great trips. They're going on fantastic spa vacations. They're making their high schools and college alma maters very happy. They're buying things for their grandchildren, or helping fund their private school and college tuitions.

They would spend lavishly in hotels, restaurants, gas stations, museums, malls, banks, car showrooms, and clothing stores—just a few examples that come to mind—if the guys in charge made these environments more female-friendly.

Frankly, I don't think the things women are asking for are all that complicated. Are you ready for the short list?

CLEANLINESS

The female of the species likes and appreciates—you might even say she *demands*—clean. It's hard-wired. "Clean" and "unclean" register for most women instantaneously. For a majority of the world's females, *Am I in a clean environment?* is an intuition, an undercurrent, a sixth sense, a vibe they pick up about every room in their house, every retail establishment they frequent, every dressing room they try clothing on in, every restaurant they dine in, every hotel room they plunk their suitcase down in, every health club they join, every swimming pool they wade into, and every bathroom they enter.

Why? If we think about it, issues of cleanliness play a natural, crucial role in female hygiene, child rearing, as well as in the acquisition and preparation of food—historically a female occupation traceable back to our earliest hunter-gatherer days. This same vigilant attention to cleanliness also finds its place in the nursing profession, which calls for close proximity to bodily fluids and waste, another historically female occupation.

Two years ago I volunteered for two nights a week at a geriatric hospital, working alongside critically ill elderly patients. It got me out of the house when I came home from work and was incredibly rewarding. An important part of our hospital training was teaching us volunteers how to wash our hands properly after making any kind of physical contact with a patient. As a male, I assumed

I'd just run my fingers under a stream of water, add soap, scrub, wash off, then dry my hands off on my jeans. Nope, here's the right way to do it: 1) with a dry paper towel, turn on the faucet; 2) soap your hands completely, while singing "Happy Birthday" (the whole thing, too); 3) rinse your hands, then turn off the faucet with the same sheet of paper towel; and 4) use that paper towel to dry your hands.

If men did that a dozen times a day, they'd appreciate the level of cleanliness that most females live with and expect every day of their lives. Clean *matters* to women—can I be any more clear? Over the course of their lives, thanks to mothers and girlfriends and wives, most men, including myself, have found this out the hard way.

CONTROL

If you are a male, perhaps you are involved with a female who insists on doing all the driving. Or, on the rare times she allows you behind the driver's seat, she spends the trip playing with the buttons that govern the heat or air conditioning. She can never get the temperature quite right. As for that song you're playing on the radio, is there a way to lower the bass any, she wonders aloud? In environments from airline terminals to malls to movie theaters to retail environments, one of the things that's stood out to me is the widespread female discomfort with the default settings installed and organized, no doubt, by a male management team.

Again, it is not that females necessarily want to change them. All they want is the option. Fair enough?

This same issue of control comes up with the concept of seating. People love movable seating. Again, not because they are in any hurry to move; they simply want to know it is possible. Today, a large section of New York's Times Square has been shut down to automobile traffic. Red, metal movable chairs have been positioned alongside a pedestrian walkway. Passersby can configure them any way they want to. In many environments or waiting zones, chairs are bolted to the floor. You can't move them without a jackhammer. Most women don't have one.

SAFETY

This one is a no-brainer men know, but don't *really* understand: most guys are physically stronger, not to mention bigger, than the average woman. Thus, females are conscious of their own personal security in ways most males really can't fathom, whether it's the lighting levels in the lobby, the burned-out bulb in the parking lot, or an apartment or hotel window that isn't locked, even if it's twelve feet up from the ground. Women often feel vulnerable. Safety may or may not be a design function, say, of a retail environment or a hotel, but the female's desire to know that she's safe and sound *does* fit neatly into Maslow's hierarchy of needs, which starts off with human physiological needs like breathing, food, water, sleep, and sex, followed closely by safety of our bodies, our health, and our resources, all the way up to the top of the pyramid, where we find creativity and problem solving.

Most of us have had the experience of standing in line behind a female who's finishing paying for an item at the cash/wrap. The cashier hands her a receipt—so why doesn't she move along? Instead of hustling out of there—and I've seen this time and time again—she begins an elaborate, almost Zen-like process of resecuring her belongings. She puts her coins inside her change purse. She places her bills or credit card back inside her wallet, then scans the receipt, before tucking it alongside the bills, or in a special receipt folder. She then replaces both her wallet and change purse (sometimes they're one and the same) back inside her handbag, then zips or buckles or seals it shut. One final glance down. Nope, she didn't drop anything.

She's ready to leave.

Would a male do this? In similar situations, with a queue forming, I've observed that men will often slide their purchases to one side to allow the person behind him to pay and get out of there. It could be some male animal collegiality, but I suspect it also has to do with the man's indifference to his own personal security. The elaborate choreography the female animal carries out before she exits a retail environment isn't just a coda to the enjoyment she's had while shopping, but an implicit sealing, and zippering up, of the transaction she's just completed. She's not being passive-aggressive; it's a safety issue.

CONSIDERATENESS

Here, I'm not talking about politeness, but about issues involving weight and muscle. Perhaps you have a female consumer inside your electronics store who would like nothing more than to purchase a large home-entertainment center, but is worried about getting it to her car or van, even though she took the seats out beforehand to accommodate the purchase. Most guys wouldn't admit they couldn't manage this process, either; but most women know full well the thing is way too heavy and cumbrous for them to manage. Where is the sign in the store that alleviates the female customer's anxiety that help is free and on the way—and that no tipping is permitted? Where is this same sign in supermarket parking lots?

As I said, overall, I really don't think the things women are asking for are all that complicated.

As one of the first males to attend Vassar College in 1970, I've been surrounded by interesting, accomplished women my whole life. Women have been friends and business acquaintances. I asked two women to marry me early in my life. Both turned me down.

In a way I feel I gave my heart away in my twenties and never got it back, which has freed me to have relationships in my life based on some kind of intellectual admiration. I'm drawn to smart, independent, accomplished women. Over the years, I've been involved with politicians and art critics, dancers and musicians. In most cases, I've stayed on very good terms with them. Both my female friends and my old girlfriends have turned into an extremely positive network for me over the years—women who've helped me advance the interests of my company, find an agent, publish books, and so on.

Though I've never married, for more than a decade I've shared my life and my living space with a female I love and admire. Her name is Sheryl, but I call her "Dreamboat." Why? She is one. One of the things that's made what we have work is that we give each other a lot of rope. A lot of the time, our schedules are in conflict. I'm on the road half the year, while Sheryl, a classical flutist, is gone evenings, performing in a long-running Broadway musical. Her time off is spent playing music festivals around the country. We don't see each other that much, but when we do, I always feel I've come home.

The wide circle of females in my life has made me realize that over the past couple of decades, the changing status of women has transformed our landscape, and the way the world is transacted—and in many cases, how far it still has to go. Women are experiencing a fundamental shift in who and what they are, and this has profound consequences for all of us. Most people don't realize the extent of it.

The thing is, I don't feel any threat to my masculinity by advocating on behalf of women. It isn't that making a retail environment more female-friendly ends up turning it somehow less male-friendly. The irony is that, by walking the female path, you end up making things better for women *and* men.

When I glance through my Rolodex, I find there are women I consider to be goddesses—women who took pioneering roles in their industries, or who have a distinct point of view concerning the shifting role of females in society. I'll be checking in with a few of them over the course of these pages. We'll use facts and figures culled from market research and secondary research wherever appropriate, including from my firm Envirosell's work. You can laugh, think about it, mull it over.

That said, I'm still no expert on gender issues. I'm just a boy writing about girls. Everybody knows all females aren't the same. There are women who love to shop, and women who can't stand the idea. Women who can march into a car dealership, make small talk with the salesguy, and walk out holding the keys to a new minivan, and women who leave it to the man in their lives to carry out the actual transaction. But I will say that there are certain commonalities that females share with other members of their gender, just as two guys who have nothing to say to each other will always have things in common.

The point is, while men were busy doing other things, women were becoming a major social, cultural, and economic force.

Take a look at how they've already transformed the everyday world.

1

HOUSEQUAKE

I'm parked in front of a large, expensive stone fence, across from a McMansion, some fifty miles north of Manhattan. You go in—I'm staying put, thank you.

Ever taken an up-close gander at a McMansion? Despite the builder's intention that the structure resemble something like Versailles, or an English countryside spread owned by an aging British rocker, the McMansions that sprout across most of the first world went up less than two decades ago. They've just been constructed to look as though they've been there forever.

As a popular, if insulting, descriptive term, "McMansion" came into being in the early 1990s, courtesy of New York environmentalist Jay Westervelt. He coined it to describe a real-estate trend that began taking root in the 1980s, when the Wall Street bull market was creating bucketfuls of newly minted wealth. A McMansion generally refers to a gaudy, oversize, spanking-new dwelling situated on a piece of land that can barely contain its size, the unfortunate result being that most McMansions stand cheek-to-jowl with their next door neighbors. Some are the result of teardowns, a repulsive contemporary epidemic whereby a pleasant, maybe historic older house is demolished—along with its plantings, backyard, and provenance—to be replaced by a dramatically out-of-proportion monstrosity that straddles the neighborhood like an . . . I don't know what. Words fail me.

As a species, the McMansion carries with it the whiff of rote, assembly-line, cookie-cutter construction, not to mention a high degree of aesthetic bankruptcy. It's also associated with new money. As the first McMansions began showing their mugs across the American and global landscapes, in no time at all they became convenient symbols not just of financial boom times, but of the male ego run amok.

As the penultimate guy dwelling, the McMansion is characterized by, among other things:

1. A schizophrenic mix-and-match of classical and neoclassical design work, ranging from French château to English to Jacobean to contemporary Cosa Nostra ("neo-eclectic" is the polite term for this architectural ragtag).

2. A bizarre assortment of roofline façades. When in doubt put up a dormer, porticos, *Gone with the Wind*-like columns, Palladian windows, phony stucco, bay windows with stone trim, and a garage spacious enough to hold half a dozen vintage cars, snowmobiles, four-wheelers, and a state-of-the-art woodworking shop that no one has ever run a lathe in.

3. No trees. No bushes. No shrubs. No vegetation anywhere save for a few shivering plantings to give the impression of vitality amid the general vibe of stale newness. From the builder's perspective, it was cheaper to denude the whole lot before breaking ground, which meant demolishing trees that had been around for centuries, giving shade and pleasure. The absence of mature plantings around most American McMansions gives them an eerie, soul-sucking quality that's just the opposite of majestic.

It's as though the most unspeakable acts imaginable were taking place behind closed doors.

4. Where's the porch? There isn't one. Porches cost too much. If one of the intentions of a porch is to provide a bridge from a family's private world to the outside world, in this neighborhood a porch would come across as overly familiar and, well, not very regal.

5. If you are a woman, the task of keeping a house this size clean would bring on a migraine a week. Just keeping track of where your family is would be next to impossible unless you outfitted them all with electronic ankle bracelets. If we think about the traditional female role within the family as that of nest maker, that same nest implies some form of focus. Inside a McMansion, the maternal role would take on another description: ensuring that the members of your brood didn't feel lonely, and simply wander off. Plus, what happens to the female wage earner who's not only working a full-time job, but who, even with a more or less equitable division of household labor, is saddled both with keeping her family's house clean and doing all the provisioning? That's a burden better off left to the imagination.

6. This isn't a characteristic, just a general observation: I want to go home. Then I remember: this *is* somebody's home. But what human being would want to live in a place like this?

7. A man. Who doesn't get it.

8. Good-bye, McMansions. And hello to a new species of home that accommodates the female of the species.

Maybe sometimes you wake up, thrashing, from a dream about the house you grew up in. Up two or three steps to a welcome mat, sodden with years of rain. The cozy inside hallway, with its generic floral wallpaper. The brown banister, the stairs with their worn carpeting, the dining room used exclusively on Thanksgiving, Christmas Eve, and whenever Grandma came to visit; the living room with Dad's special chair.

The kitchen sat in the back of the house. From the fridge to that stove with its gray hard coils, the appliances had white marshmallowlike contours. You couldn't even see where or how the fridge opened, plastered as it was with all manner of family stuff—Polaroid pics of Dad on the fourteenth tee, the family reunion in Colonial Williamsburg, a small calendar courtesy of the local hardware store, ladybug magnets, and of course, artwork drawn, sketched, and finger-painted by the kindergarten-age Picassos in the house.

Sure, it was cramped, but it was home. And upstairs, you could probably find a single master bedroom with an attached bath for Mom and Dad, plus two smaller rooms for the kids.

In today's market, a house like that probably wouldn't sell.

When my parents bought a house in Chevy Chase, Maryland, in 1964, the property they bought cost roughly my father's annual salary. When I give a speech, I like to say that if a person lives in a house equal to his or her annual salary in 2010, I'm not entirely sure whether to be sympathetic or envious. The point is, it takes two incomes today to sustain a middle-class lifestyle. During World War II, Rosie the Riveter rolled up her sleeves for the good cause while the men risked their lives on the front, but over the past few decades, women have gone to work to ensure there's a roof and more over their families' heads. Along the way, the traditional female role as homemaker has morphed into that of home designer, home contractor, tool-belt lady, and, in many cases, direct mortgage holder.

So what does the twenty-first-century housing unit typically look like—or rather, one that might attract a handful of excited bids?

I'll tell you this much: It won't look like the house you grew up in.

* * *

The American home hasn't altered its basic design since the 1950s. The changes we're starting to see—after years of protest, I might add—have been readjusted to accommodate certain cultural and demographic realities. Houses that suit a nontraditional family sell at a premium these days. Two master bedrooms, for example, for two sisters living together; enough space for adult children; three generations living under one roof; an apartment for Grandma, or maybe for a local grad student who helps with the cooking and cleaning and dog walking in exchange for room and board.

Nearly a third of all empty nesters anticipate downsizing or simplifying their lifestyles. More and more home buyers are amenable to giving up square footage in exchange for a house containing things they actually use—someplace smaller, more containable, better fit-to-scale. Perhaps a house in a nearby university town, where they can take advantage of classes, movies, theater, coffee shops, and bookstores. Good-bye, male-oriented house—now say hello to a dwelling that accommodates the specific needs of the gender who's actually in charge of running the thing: the female.

For example, there might be a home office, or a home exercise room. The house might feature a stand-alone apartment with its own fridge, freezer, and dishwasher. If there's an in-ground swimming pool, there could be a separate bar-keeping station outside, as well as a rolling cabinet for plates and cups. Gabriel and Miranda, my teenage niece and nephew, have their own miniature domestic setups in their bedrooms—small fridges for sodas and snacks. It's not that they're spoiled rotten—it's just that my sister won't buy them certain things they like to crunch on or guzzle (like Red Bull), so she makes them buy and store it themselves.

As the nuclear family gets smaller, one element of the American landscape is the idea of multiple generations all living under one roof, grandkids in one wing, grandparents in another. With more and more adult children living at home or, having had a taste of the real world, slinking back to the security of their childhood bedrooms, I'm intrigued by the idea of a bedroom that has its own door to the outside. A conventional house, of course, has a front door and a back door and perhaps a side door leading off a mudroom. But who's to say that as our houses evolve, they may not end up taking on more and more doors?

(Imagine that you're a twenty-six-year-old male or female and you've returned to live at home. You would very much appreciate the option of passing back and forth to your bedroom without passing through a suite of more formal living spaces, not to mention prying eyes. Barring shimmying up the fire escape, a separate door would be nice.)

This reparceling of rooms is particularly true for Hispanic and Latino boomers, whose parents often discourage them from leaving home. Latino boomers are also enmeshed with their grandchildren and aging parents in a way non-Latino families aren't. For example, it's a sure thing that every single Latino vacation will include members of all generations. In response, the Princess Cruise line has tailored some of its accommodations for the multigenerational family group at sea.

Alternately, more than a few suburbanites are saying, "To heck with rural living—let's move back to a more happening urban environment." I get the arguments against aging in a city like New York or Chicago, but I also see the advantages. Me, I'll take the ability to walk to Lincoln Center, someone else shoveling the front of my West Village floor-thru, and home delivery of a boxful of cheese from Murray's Cheese Shop.

Contributing to our mobility, as a society we've entered an era of disposable everything. Ikea and H&M have given us permission, or at least justification, to throw out and redecorate. Both these stores sell items that are good, cheap, and not meant to last.

Speaking of "not meant to last," perhaps new homeowners should begin thinking of their houses as transformational. How long do they plan on living there? If the answer were forever, they'd be wise, as I said, to take into account the changing future status of their children, their parents, and their grandchildren. This is simply known as planning your life up front. I compare this to the plight of friends in New York who've lived for years in rent-stabilized apartments, and who are effectively denied the possibility of ever moving. How could they? Their monthly rent would quadruple overnight. They're married to their rent-stabilized apartments, a housing choice that's predetermined the rest of their lives.

Another point about downsizing: Our recent economic woes, as well as the decluttering that many baby boomers are either doing, or planning on doing, has focused our attention on stuff, namely, how much of it we've accumulated over the years. Is it any coincidence that over the past thirty years, as we've overleveraged our credit cards and bought three large-screen TVs rather than the single one we really need, that the self-storage industry has become one of the fastest-growing sectors of the U.S. commercial real-estate industry? There are roughly 53,000 primary self-storage facilities ("primary" meaning that self-storage is the main source of business revenue). Industry grosses as of 2007 were approximately $22.1 billion. One in ten households currently rents a self-storage unit, which represents an increase of approximately 65 percent over the past twelve years. Total self-storage rentable space in the United States is now 2.21 billion square feet—that's seventy-eight square miles of space overall. Sure, a lot of these minigarages are rented to transient military personnel, but an even greater number are rented to civilian men and women who've moved more than once, or who've inherited furniture and paintings from their parents and grandparents they just don't know what to do with.

It's little wonder that container stores are doing such booming business these days. Even during an economic slowdown, the female religion of keeping things neat and tidy isn't going anywhere.

In 2007, a Utah-based neighborhood development group known as Kennecott Land introduced several concepts that they thought female home buyers would be looking for in a contemporary home. The board was made up of female architects and female home buyers, but men, I'm pretty sure, would appreciate some of these touches, too. To wit:

A kitchen that in some fashion includes or otherwise incorporates the children. Ideally, this consists of a kitchen with multilevel counters that opens out onto a spacious play area. That way, the kitchen isn't just a dedicated temple for whipping up smoothies or nachos, but also the place where, as you're preparing dinner, you can keep an eye on the Legos, the American Girl dollhouse, the websites the kids are attempting to access on the family computer, and whether or not the lamp handed down by Great-Aunt Winnie is about to shatter.

An added benefit? By showing that Mom and Dad have been running a small restaurant for years, it might penetrate the children's heads just how fortunate they are. Here's another possibility: the children can cook alongside their parents, learn how to flip an omelet, make a pot of tea, melt cheese onto a hamburger, or cook linguine *al dente*. Better still, they can do it at a counter that's not too high, and that allows them enough room to mince, grate, peel, blend, purify, sauté, and bake to their heart's content. Meal preparation is thus cut in half—well, ideally—and if the kitchen is big enough for more than two people, cooking as a team can be a gas.

Another concept Kennecott's female market advisory board came up with was the idea of the family bathroom. No, not one tiny cupboard where the entire family empties their bladders at the same time in name-tagged stalls, but a pair of side-to-side bathrooms separated by a door. That way, Mom and Dad can take turns showering and brushing their teeth in the morning while affording them a glimpse of what's going on in the next room as the kids suit up for school. The door can be shut tight or kept ajar, depending on the time of day, and who needs to do what when. No adult I know wants their kids to ogle them while they're showering or bathing. And after a certain age, the same goes for kids. Everyone's happy.

Intriguing stuff, and better still, formulated by women who know how females want to live, as well as reclaim their own houses.

One of the great villains of the twentieth century was Frank Lloyd Wright. That Americans were able to move to a suburban culture far away from our neighbors estranged us from the village community and mentality that I consider intrinsic to human nature. The very male decision of "I want this piece of turf, where I can drive to my job" became the dominant trope, whereas the female of the couple often found herself parked in the castle, unfamiliar with her neighbors or feeling completely cut off, particularly if she had children.

Is it any wonder the New Urbanist Community has become another alternative for today's female—particularly the single mother?

New Urbanist Communities, a mixture of city and suburb, have thrived across the United States. There are probably fifty or so examples, the best known being Seaside. Seaside is located in Florida, close by a beach, and is like a perfect Hollywood town—clean, orderly, with shops and services, anything from bike repair to medical offices—situated within the actual community. At Seaside, there are three art galleries and seventeen restaurants, pizza and pottery parties, sand castle-building tournaments, even a repertory theater. One of the appeals of a New Urbanist Community is that there is always someone looking out for everyone. It also means many incidents have a tendency *not* to happen—like domestic violence and crime. Security is implicit and largely moot: Rather than residents feeling obliged to hire a security company, one of their neighbors will tell them she saw someone suspicious eyeing the house, or that she signed for a FedEx package.

For a single mother, childcare is a huge and expensive issue. But within a New Urbanist Community, the orientation of the community is such that everyone is overseeing everyone else's children.

They can tell Mom if Jimmy had a bike accident or was smoking cigarettes in the bushes. Thus, the single mother has a number of built-in safety valves that come free with the choice she made to move there. How many apartment buildings or suburban subdivisions can say the same?

Moreover, community residents can surrender their reliance on their cars and walk where they need to go. Friends of mine who've left cities for the suburbs tell me that walking—the sheer exercise involved in daily living—is one of the top three things they miss most about living in a city.

The downside to living within a New Urbanist Community is a certain homogeneity to the different types of houses, as well as to the strictures governing community living. If you want to paint your house purple with polka dots, chances are you'll be told you can't. And because of the lack of density, while the communities themselves may feature everything from a dry cleaner to seven different apparel stores, retail hasn't quite caught up yet with the surrounding towns.

But it will.

So how has today's busy, multitasking female resculpted the contemporary home in her own image? Let's take a look. We'll go from room to room, from the kitchen to the bathroom, to the home office to the home gym, before we make our way to that universal home away from home, the hotel. From there, we'll shop for electronics, visit the topic of females and sin, visit a department store, stroll the mall, stop by a farmers' market, peruse a drugstore, explore the world of beauty and hair, and, finally, end up online.

We can't cover everything, but I hope you enjoy where we end up.

2

DON'T PHUNK WITH MY HEARTH

I'm standing inside one of the most gorgeous kitchens I've ever seen. The double-wide refrigerator gleams. The stove has eight burners. There's a separate wine cooler, an espresso machine, a rice cooker, a popcorn maker, and a blender powerful enough to make smoothies. I don't ever want to go home.

Two decades ago, most women might not even have known that a high-end kitchen store even existed. Today, a middle-class woman from the middle of the country not only knows about Williams-Sonoma, but has access to the latest bathroom and kitchen designs and fashions thanks to the Internet, shelter magazines, and twenty-four-hour cable television with programs like *This Old House, Why Don't We Flip This Joint?, Design That Stylin' Crib,* and *Cook This Junk for Dinner in Five Seconds* (all right, except for *This Old House,* I made up the other three).

Until the end of the Mesolithic era, the female may have been best known as a gatherer and forager, a gender which derived immense pleasure from the art of scavenging. But today, gathering isn't just about the acquisition of food—it's about what happens to that food once the female totes it back to her lair: the contemporary kitchen.

For the female of the species, the contemporary kitchen is a place where she can wander euphorically among a showroom of gadgets, fixtures, and appliances. Just as a man collects his toys—the all-terrain vehicle, the Harley, or the vintage, seldom-used Porsche he keeps sheeted in one side of the garage—the kitchen has been transformed into the arena where the female can compensate for all the male gadgets under the roof. It's as if she's saying, "Hey, if you have the power saw and the new MacBook Pro, I want an incredible refrigerator!"

The kitchens most of us grew up in were drably utilitarian in nature. They were rooms where we went to eat, grab a snack, or pack a box lunch. The kitchen was hardly the red-hot center of the house, or a place where you and your family would ever want to flock, cluster, congregate, converse, or hang out. Certainly it wasn't ever a playground for Mom.

What killed that old, utilitarian kitchen after it had been around for centuries? Before the Civil War, a female who oversaw a household took it upon herself to cook, mend, wash, and make candles in a kitchen typically dominated by a giant fireplace hearth. It was her room, but it was also her *work*room. It wasn't until the Victorian era that technology began to make its presence known. By the middle of the nineteenth century, the first cast-iron stoves fired by coal or wood were flooding the urban markets, followed by their appearance into more rural areas. Kitchens of the post-Civil War era were downsized to accommodate the mass exodus of household servants who'd decided a better, and better-paid, life was available to them in the factories. Almost as if responding to the disappearance of human bodies, the first ever labor-saving gadgets started showing up.

The period between the 1880s and the turn of the twentieth

century might be considered the Golden Age of the kitchen appliance. It was then that a slew of kitchen doodads that most of us take for granted today overwhelmed the consumer market as never before. The result was the creation of the first mechanized kitchen, one that freed the stay-at-home female of that era from the servitude that most had considered the be-all and end-all of their lives.

Toasters, egg beaters, waffle irons, electric *thises* and *thats*. By the 1920s a female consumer could buy anything from a vacuum cleaner to a washing machine or an iron—not to mention the standard Hoosier cabinet, a six-foot pine workstation featuring bins, drawers for silverware, and a solid wood surface for chopping and dicing.

It could be argued that with the advent of appliances, architects began building kitchens around appliances, rather than the other way around. By the 1930s, with the fridge and stove in place, the kitchen was now planned and adorned as carefully and lovingly as any other room in the house. In the 1940s, the suburbs took the lead, employing the latest in assembly-line kitchen technology. In Levittown, William Levitt transposed the kitchen from the back of the house to the front via the premise that a kitchen situated up front could serve as the unofficial domestic control center of a contemporary home.

Mechanization was fast and furious. Good-bye, garbage can; hello, trash disposal. Farewell, oven; hello, microwave. And that was just the beginning.

Still, it wasn't until the 1970s and 1980s when women began going to work en masse that the kitchen became more integrated into the rest of the house. If a female came home tired from work and immediately set to work preparing a meal for her family, she didn't want to be sequestered in a remote corner of the house. Rather, she wanted the kitchen to blend openly and harmoniously with the rest of the house—Dad in the living room with his pipe and newspaper, while the kids fooled around under one of the wings of the dining room table.

In the intervening years, even without a literal hearth and fire blazing away in the contemporary kitchen, the kitchen has morphed into what is today the social center of the contemporary home—no longer just a functional part of a house, but a showcase of beauty and design.

And social centers should be outfitted accordingly, which means, in some cases, the advent of cutting-edge appliances, ranging from dual-fuel Viking ranges to Sub-Zero fridges to granite counters whose price, in many cases, could send a child to a good state university for a year. The Williams-Sonoma store in New York's Time Warner Center features two $30,000 stoves. Not even the head chef at Buckingham Palace needs a $30,000 stove. Think of it as the female equivalent of the Hummer: some women just like owning it.

Let's have a look at this monster fridge.

The refrigerator has trumped the stove as the kitchen's seminal appliance. One way to look at it is that everyone—Mom, Dad, and the kids—finds their way into the fridge, while only a select few touch the stove. Contemporary refrigerator design has been influenced both by a *Real Simple* sense of order, as well as by the Green movement, the underlying thesis being that as more and more women work, having time-saving devices in the kitchen helps the contemporary female multitask. Today, ironically, with microwavable meals and bagged, prewashed salads, the kitchen has never been more overdesigned—or less used. It's the place where women go when they have the time to cook (emphasis on *when* they have the time). Having it, and knowing it's there, is an integral part of the reward for working outside the home.

The present-day American notion of the kitchen as Command Central, with the female of the house as the captain in the cockpit, isn't necessarily the case in other countries, where the widespread images coming from the Western European and American fashion and shelter magazines are, at best, irrelevant. Most middle-class women in emerging markets have cooks and maids. The kitchen doesn't serve the same public role as it does in America and Western Europe. The notion of entertaining in your kitchen or taking pride in your skills as a skilled gourmet cook is out of the question in those countries. Overseas kitchens have evolved differently, based on local cultural issues, diets, and space limitations.

The Japanese dishwasher, for example, is a tabletop fixture. The ideal graduation gift for a Japanese female isn't a new computer and printer, but an assortment of color-coordinated appliances. This gift not only helps nudge the young female out of the house but recognizes her right to start her adult life living alone. The Japanese have also come up with a line of appliances for the single woman that allows her to dry her intimate apparel in her own kitchen, saving her the embarrassment of hanging them outdoors in plain sight.

In America, we've seen more and more so-called open-plan kitchens—kitchens that blend seamlessly into dens or other sprawling rooms. Simultaneously, this has meant that kitchen appliances have had to be miniaturized (otherwise they'll overwhelm the overall aesthetic), hence the trend toward the kind of space-saving design that was once limited to small, boxcar-size urban apartments, or boats. These include under-the-counter microwaves, warming drawers, in-cabinet coffee makers and espresso machines, and very often an LCD TV either angled into a cabinet for optimal viewing capacity, or built into the fridge itself, so the female of the house can catch the *Today* show while waiting for the morning coffee to finish brewing.

Of course, on the high end, there's the megakitchen, too. These kitchens are so cavernous they have an assortment of dedicated zones, each with its own suite of similar appliances—a fridge, an oven, a sink, a cook top. There might be a water station—a rotating food preparation unit that permits anywhere from four to six cooks to work over two sinks and two separate cutting boards. There could be a supersonic oven, in which heated air gusts through food at speeds of sixty miles per hour, which permits the home chef to prepare meals roughly fifteen times faster than she could using a conventional oven. Appliance gurus have even come out with an "intelligent" oven that begins cooking your chicken or Thanksgiving turkey with a single call from your mobile phone.

Nowadays, women are also being exposed to devices that show them that if they buy this or that, they'll be transformed instantly into kitchen heroines. I'm talking about kitchen scales, Cuisinarts, industrial blenders, miniblenders, minichoppers, juicers, smoothie makers, popcorn poppers, pizza-making accessories, not to mention skimmers, peelers, mortars, pestles, spoons, spatulas, spice racks, tongs, steamers, timers, pepper mills, salt mills, lemon and lime squeezers, ladles, spatter screens, salad spinners, whisks, thermometers, strainers, colanders, bottle openers, can openers, jar openers, basters, basting brushes, graters, shredders, pancake molds, knife blocks, knife sharpeners . . .

We love you, Mom.

Just like the new rooms we're seeing in the contemporary home, today's kitchen appliances have everything to do with saving labor—shortening the time it takes to do anything. In the kitchen, we're passing through the era of the short cut, as if to mimic the efficiency level of the fast-food joints many of us grew up frequenting. Many studies prove that time spent in the kitchen has plummeted since the mid-1960s, back when American women spent a weekly average of thirteen hours boiling and broiling. Today, U.S. women confess to devoting roughly thirty minutes a day to food preparation. One expert has posited a connection between the drop in home cooking and the United States' soaring obesity rate, given that just about any kitchen-produced meal is healthier than its fast-food equivalent. Which is why in the United Kingdom, where obesity rates are closing in on those of Americans', the British government recently passed a law mandating secondary-school students to attend cooking classes.

If the idea of kitchen preparation has become one of amphetaminelike efficiency, Ron Popeil, perhaps the most successful TV huckster in history, is the modern-day god of getting-it-done-and-quickly-too. Any female who flicks on the TV on Sunday morning or late at night is almost certain to find Ron proudly showing off his latest revolutionary, time-saving invention, whether it's the Showtime Rotisserie ("Just set it, and forget it!"), the Chop-O-

Matic hand food processor ("All your onions chopped to perfection without shedding a single tear!"), the Dial-O-Matic ("Slice a tomato so thin it only has one side!"), the Inside-the-Shell Egg Scrambler ("Gets rid of those slimy egg whites in your scrambled eggs!"), the Electric Food Dehydrator ("Instead of giving kids candy, give them apple snacks or banana chips! And it's great if you're a hunter, fisherman, backpacker, or camper. Makes beef jerky for around three dollars a pound, and you know what went in it, because you made it yourself!"), and the Solid Flavor Injection (which, though lacking a catchy tag line, has always looked suspiciously to me like the act of artificial human impregnation).

In case you were wondering, infomercials' target audience is the female.

Then there's the mandolin.

Me? I'm in love with my mandolin.

Not the fretted wooden instrument related to the lute family (I've never once shown my face at a Renaissance faire), but the contemporary kitchen appliance. I love my mandolin so much I keep it in the top drawer of my kitchen cabinet next to my wine corkscrew. As a kitchen tool, the mandolin is simplicity itself—a knife blade affixed onto a plastic holding mechanism. The fancier ones offer a choice of different blades that can accommodate whatever it is you're slicing. Let's say I'm in a stir-fry mood, and I want to chop up an onion, a bell pepper, and a couple of potatoes. My mandolin allows me to slice up each vegetable incredibly quickly and thinly. I place my veggies into the microwave and ten minutes later, I've produced a semielegant, healthy, one-dish meal.

The only trouble is that if you're not careful with the mandolin, your fingertips can go flying. That hasn't happened to mine yet.

For women starved for time, fast and easy does it. Cookbook author, TV personality, and all-around spokesperson Rachael Ray has built an empire based on cooking decent, wholesome meals in no time at all—thirty minutes max, usually. Just as contemporary appliances are all about saving time, today's cookbook divas are all about speed and corner-cutting. It's as if they're engaged in a race to create the most edible (or at least edible-looking) meal in the shortest time possible.

Where does the male fit inside this new world of appliances and gadgets?

Cast your mind backward to, say, 1975. A group of men is hunkered around the kitchen table. They could be blue-collar, white-collar, or no-collar. Ask them to lay their hands faceup or facedown on the table. Take a look. I can guarantee you that fully one half of these guys will bear traces of residual grease on their fingers from working with their hands on car engines, car hoods, exhaust pipes, and what have you.

Like most young men of my generation, I was taught early on how to change my car's oil and spark plugs. That was kind of the deal—now that the state and your parents have entrusted you with a driver's license, you'd better know how to change your own oil, because no one else is going to do it for you. But by the early eighties, that deafening, slamming noise you heard around the country was the sound of millions of car hoods closing forever. Then, as now, the car engine has been fully digitalized, and off-limits to the drivers of those cars, that is, if they want to honor their warranties. Until recently I owned an Audi I called Greta. Greta was eight years old, had about 75,000 miles on her odometer, and I just traded her in for a newer model. I can count the number of times I ever opened her hood either to take a look-see, or to tinker with or fix something. Not just because I live in New York City, and the opportunities for getting my hands dirty with an engine or spark plugs are limited. It's because my Audi service agreement was rendered null and void if I went so far as to lay a pinkie inside.

Which leaves my hands—and the hands of males everywhere!—grappling for stuff to do! Boxing—it's too late for that. Backgammon—I'm not the type. The thing is, men like to do stuff for themselves. And if we're not always welcome in the kitchen, except every now and again, there's a place for us: outdoors.

Which is where the backyard barbecue comes into play. I don't just mean a Weber grill with charcoal briquettes, a can of lighter fluid, and a match. No, I'm talking about those big gas-lit barbecues, the ones with oversize stainless-steel spit rods and spit forks hanging off one side, as if men were smoking fisher cats rather than chicken breasts or hot dogs or steaks. There's nothing even remotely feminine about this setup. It involves raw flesh, uncontrolled flames, smoke, heat, weaponry, patience, nerves, and vigilance. Plus, the specs on some of these machines are designed to rock a man's world. One gas grill that recently came to my attention delivers 78,000 BTUs over an enormous cooking surface, as well as a recessed rotisserie burner, a heavy-duty rotisserie and motor kit, a smoke hood, dual internal halogen lamps imbedded in that same smoke hook, a built-in LCD digital meat and grill thermometer, and a stainless-steel valve manifold.

Nostalgic for that feeling of grease on your hands? You've just gotten it back.

Men want—rather, *need*—arenas where they can get their hands dirty. If Rachael Ray is the reigning queen of speed cooking, for men, the culinary equivalent is Bobby Flay, host of TV's *Grill It!*, *Throwdown with Bobby Flay,* and *Boy Meets Grill*—or Emeril Lagasse with his cries of "*Bam!*" and "Kick it up a notch!" or *Iron Chef America,* in which mostly male chefs have sixty minutes to improvise a multicourse meal focused around a single-themed ingredient. There's a winner and a loser (just as men like). In this case, speed and efficiency don't have to do with freeing up time to spend with your family, but with besting your opponent. Tell guys all you want that some of the best chefs on earth are male. Typically they'll shrug: *whatever.* These cooking shows have given men a familiarity and a facility with heavy iron skillets bordering on affection—some of these black-bottomed pans could almost double as free weights! The result being that slowly, and in their own ways, men are overcoming the idea that being facile, improvisational, or even adept in a kitchen is somehow an affront to their masculinity.

That's a good thing.

3

LET US SPRAY

For today's frazzled female, it's the ultimate inner sanctum. Think luxury day spa, minus the attendants, the hiking trails, or any obligation to tip the staff. If she has children, it's the one space in her house where she can be truly, gloriously alone and private. Best of all, the bathroom has shed its historical associations as a vaguely shameful destination that no woman wanted to be observed visiting.

Quite the opposite, in fact.

Thanks to women, the bathroom has come a long way from its humble origins.

The present-day master bathroom has become a space where hedonism, fantasy, luxury, and self-regard (sometimes even a touch of self-adoration) collude in a miasma of mist, steam, fragrance, occasional candlelight, and a sense of delicious, unhurried aloneness. As a species, we've evolved from a sealed, miniaturized unit tucked under the back stairwell to a room more akin to a rain forest with an attached toilet. These days, the rule as far as bathrooms are concerned is the More the Merrier. One in four houses constructed in 2005, in fact, featured three or more. In most middle-class homes across the United States, the basic footprint of the bathroom has gotten larger over the past several decades.

Knowing that this is the era of the glorious bathroom, I checked in with Billie Brenner, the founder of Billie Brenner Ltd, the top-of-the-line dealer of high-end bathroom and kitchen hardware in the American Northeast. Brands like Lulu, Belle de Jour, Jado—Billie sells only the best from her showroom in the Boston Design Center.

"Billie," I say, "what did the typical bathroom look like before places like Billie Brenner Limited came along?"

Billie says, "It was *completely* utilitarian."

That's an understatement. In its earliest incarnations, the bathroom was a forbidden, whispered-about space. Because of its unseemly reputation, the early development of the bathroom was largely driven by the desire to reduce it to the smallest possible dimensions—to miniaturize this most necessary of rooms, to create dollhouse-size quarters for adults. The first-ever bathrooms were tucked away inside dressing rooms and off upstairs bedrooms. It was considered wasteful and possibly immoral to allot excess space to what was seen as the most quotidian (and politely unpublicized) of human needs. Why draw attention?

The powder room—also referred to as a guest bathroom, or half bath—dates back to the early eighteenth century. Again, it was a room no larger than a closet where men and women retreated to get their wigs repowdered. The powder room endured through the Victorian era. Proper ladies of the time would excuse themselves, rise, and announce that they were going to "go powder their noses." Women of a certain background and generation still employ this charming turn of phrase. The small, windowless, often eaved powder room lasts to this day, sequestered under countless stairwells, permitting visitors to use the facilities without having to trespass into the upstairs inner sanctums of their hosts.

I have a friend who for a decade lived in an elegant, sprawling, 120-year-old Federal-style house in New England. The place was ideal in every way, except it lacked a first-floor bathroom. For many houses constructed in that era, a downstairs bathroom, even a tiny powder room, was considered both an exception and an indiscretion. Certainly no early-twentieth-century female wished to be seen entering one. Whenever my friend and his wife had company, the guests were obliged to trudge upstairs, where they were then faced with a puzzling choice: to use the bathroom halfway down the hall, or directly beside it, separated by a hallway door, a second, narrower bathroom designed originally for the servants, who lived in the nether quarters of the house. In the beginning, my friend found the absence of a downstairs bathroom appealingly quirky, but over time, the sheer inconvenience started to annoy him. Late at night, if he was feeling lazy or antagonistic, he would pee into the bushes off the back porch.

Today it's a far different story. "For a female, a bathroom reflects two things," Billie remarks. "Number one is her comfort. Number two is how highly she thinks of herself."

So when did we make the transition from the bathroom as a utilitarian fixture to an oasis of self-renewal? The simplest answer is that human beings, and technological efficiency, evolved over time. As a species we went from being able to have hot water in our homes to being able to use appliances. Not very long ago, most bathrooms lacked electrical outlets. Money, and lots of it, played a part as well. When a married couple was done fixing up a beautiful master bedroom, it often followed naturally that they needed an equally good-looking bathroom, too.

Another driving factor behind the design and the amenities in the contemporary bathroom is the fact that more and more people have traveled, both domestically and internationally. A visit to Italy. A weekend jaunt south of the border. A road trip to Santa Fe. What is propelling many consumers to buy better quality and better design? Their own aesthetic education. America is known for being a footloose culture. Few people have their children, or their parents, living in a single concentrated area. The number of people today who've visited the American Southwest and stumbled across tilework they loved, or the Pacific Northwest, where they fell hard for wood and glass, is substantial.

A few years ago I was working in DubaiLand, a theme park in Dubai. The company that hired me had imported a slew of designers to work on the place, some of whom had worked for Disney. I remember having a hard time getting across to some of these people that in many Arab countries, a child is in his teens before he's ever flushed his own toilet. There are also Middle Eastern adolescents who have never bathed themselves. Someone else has always soaped them, scrubbed them, and toweled them off.

Just consider the evolution of soap in our own U.S. bathrooms. Many of us now have several varieties, for several purposes, too. There's a squirt bottle so we can sanitize our hands during the day. Many women keep a separate bar of soap to be used exclusively on their complexions. An all-purpose bar of soap sits in the tub or shower. For teenagers and college-age males, body wash and shower gel have replaced Irish Spring and Ivory. I think of this as a trickle-down effect from the female of the species.

We may think we're addicted to the cult of clean in America, but when the Japanese visit the United States, many of them are appalled by our sanitary habits. They're aware that Americans have a distinctive smell and consider our bathing habits to be inadequate. I have Japanese colleagues who won't consider staying the night in an American hotel if it lacks a bathtub. For the Japanese, bathing is ritualistic. Most bathrooms in Japan have a drain in the middle of the floor. Japanese men and women wash themselves thoroughly before stepping inside the tub, where they lounge for a long time. In Japan, the tub is a place for repose and meditation, a place where both women and men can savor the heat, steam, and quiet. It's a purification ritual that's seeded in the Shinto philosophy. By Western standards, the water temperature is scaldingly hot. The Japanese dub those fellow countrymen and women who are addicted to bathing "ofuroholics," and the state of euphoria these tub addicts hope to attain is called *yudedako,* which translates roughly to "boiled octopus."

In Japan, they even publish a magazine designed to be read in the tub. The magazine has an inflatable device attached to it so none of the pages get soaked.

Whenever I visit Japan, I take great pains with my own personal hygiene. I'm mindful to take a hot bath every day. If I'm wearing a suit of clothes for more than twenty-four hours, I'll steam that suit daily. My goal is to be "Japanese clean." It's an important factor in their acceptance of me. I go easy on the aftershave, or avoid it entirely. I know that as a meat eater, rather than a fish eater, even if I take a dozen baths, as a *gaijin* I carry a hint of the stockyard with me. All of us are products not only of our personal hygiene habits, but of our diets. In a homogenous country, the natives smell good to one another. But when foreigners make an appearance, they tend to announce themselves first by their fragrance.

The Japanese bath has much in common with the Islamic *hamam*, or Turkish bath, which in turn is a descendant of the Roman thermal baths. Rather than serving as temples to hedonism, the *hamam* reflects the repose and serenity of Muslim culture. Architecturally, the *hamam* is laid out in a cruciform shape. A majestic dome slopes over your head. The lighting is muted, there's steam everywhere as well as a pleasant feeling of austerity. A bather gets his skin scrubbed with a glove by an attendant, followed by a head-to-toe massage. In the women's *hamam,* an attendant uses a sugar mixture to eliminate any unwanted hair, followed by henna for coloring and flower-scented water to purify the skin. Finally, a bather sits there in quietude, waiting for her body to return groggily to its senses.

The fact of the matter is that females have elevated not just the contemporary kitchen, but the bathroom, into places that both recognize and salute their status. I suspect, too, that many of the accoutrements of today's bathrooms are driven by the notes and touches installed by hotel and restaurant designers and architects. In the Hong Kong nightclub Felix, men urinate against a glass wall overlooking the city. At the Royalton Hotel, a 1980s Manhattan hot spot, men were obliged to pee, side-by-side, into a flowing waterfall—a deliberately subversive design touch for a gender accustomed since boyhood to averting their eyes from one another's genitals. Some establishments have tacked on a naughtiness factor, too. At the W Hotel in Montréal, only a wall separates the bedroom and the bathroom. Within that same wall is an eye-size cut-out hole, so you can peer at your mate showering or peeing, if you want to. And if you have a small or even medium-size exhibitionistic streak, the Hotel on Rivington in lower Manhattan offers a shower whose floor-to-ceiling windows afford pedestrians the opportunity to ogle your soapy body.

If you're feeling shy or self-conscious, the management is happy to provide blinds.

The bare minimum for today's high-end bathroom is a spa tub of some kind—despite the fact that in America, at least, the shower is more popular than the bathtub. Some of today's tubs offer females small ledges to cut their toenails or shave their legs. (One reason, I'm guessing, behind the popularity of outdoor hot tubs is that they cleanly separate the act and art of relaxation from the everyday rituals and responsibilities associated with the house.)

That said, men and women diverge dramatically when it comes to concepts of ablution and cleanliness. A good analogy is that when a man goes into a store's dressing room with a piece of clothing, and it fits—boom, he'll buy it, whereas a female can derive a great deal of pleasure from the act of playing dress-up.

This same difference between men's and women's shopping habits extends to their linger time in the bathroom. If you think about the male and female animal, how many more things does a female do in the bathroom than a man does? Let me count the ways. If you made a list—applying makeup, leg and armpit shaving, cleaning, exfoliating and moisturizing her skin, shampooing her hair, applying conditioner, studying her face in the mirror—the female wins hands down.

I can't help but be reminded of an interesting assignment Envirosell recently carried out in Japan. We were studying small personal appliances, including razor blades. Among the things we concluded, one was fairly obvious: the male relationship to hair management and removal is far different from the female's relationship to the same process. With men, there's typically a sense of pride that comes from shaving his chin, or trimming his beard or finessing his moustache. For the female consumer, hair removal is typically not something to celebrate. Whether it's on her legs or under her arms, hair is something most women want to get rid of, period. Included among our findings were that female shoppers were a) less likely to be shopping only for themselves; b) far more likely than men to purchase disposable razors; and c) less interested in blade count and more focused on product design. Guys, on the other hand, were far more brand-loyal than women, and loved that extra, stubble-slicing blade—the Mach 3 Turbo! The Quattro!—and couldn't have cared less about package design.

Among the recommendations we made was that female hair removal products, including razors, be installed not beside the men's section, but somewhere within the lingerie section—so that the act of smoothing and moisturizing a pair of female legs is detached from machismo and utilitarianism, and realigned with sensuality.

In my own home, it recently came to my attention—after more than ten years of living there—that with the exception of the master bedroom bathroom, our two other bathrooms have tiny sinks and no shelves. Our architect, come to think of it, was male. There is no place for storage. Storage is another element females bring into the equation of the contemporary bathroom: a cabinet that can hold extra rolls of toilet paper, a drawer dedicated to cosmetics and face serums, a second filled with wipes and cotton balls, a third filled with hair clips and scrunchies, a fourth filled with emergency first-aid stuff, a fifth filled with . . .

I could go on, but I don't have room.

4

NICE WORK IF YOU CAN GET IT

Let's take a glance at today's home office. But before we stick our heads in, it might be instructive to cast a glance back at our own parents' command centers.

If they had one, and if I'm remembering right, Mom's and Dad's home offices were boxy, airless places, crowded with extraneous Mom and Dad stuff. Clumsy gun-gray file drawers that had fallen off their casters and never been rolled back into position. An old Singer sewing machine, or a KLH record player or, depending on the era, an IBM Selectric or a first-generation Macintosh computer. Stacks of books, scattered pell-mell, giving off the delicious odor that passing years impart to book leather. And underneath all those papers and binders and bowls of thumbtacks and paper clips and pens and pencils and junk and mess and pure, utter Mom-and-Dad-ness, somewhere, you could have sworn, there sat a black rotary phone with a cord that twisted and tangled like an umbilicus.

The only possible way you could find the thing was if it rang.

Poor Dad, poor Mom. Like teenagers, they used their home

offices as in-house getaways. During cocktail hour, or after dinner, they might gingerly close the door, fully expecting the other occupants of the house to respect their privacy. And if you knocked politely, or simply cracked the door open an inch to ask a question or blurt out a general observation, funny, but they didn't seem all that glad to see you.

Why? Because with all due respect, their home offices were where Mom and Dad went so they could escape you. Sorry—the truth hurts.

Things have changed since then.

Beginning in 2005, according to a survey released by the American Institute of Architects, the home office topped homeowners' requests as part of the design of their houses—a desire for flexibility driven not just by rising gas prices but by a fall in technology prices and a jump in technological options. The home office was also an element of homeowners' overall interest in low-maintenance, open, multipurpose floor plans, as well.

When you think about it, by saving the contemporary female a commute to work, the home office is a means of exporting the external world into her domestic domain. Via her desktop or laptop computer and a fast Internet connection, the outside world comes to her. Personally and professionally, it's like getting takeout delivered every day of the week. If she wants, she can check the Dow Jones average, glimpse the ten-day weather forecast, set an alarm clock that can signal when the TV show she loves is about to begin, or when the oven should be turned off. It's about having the whole world—including her family—at her fingertips and within her general purview.

That's because the contemporary home office, unlike, perhaps, her own parents', is a welcoming, *mi casa es su casa* kind of space. The kind of room most women would actually *prefer* their kids to hang out in, provided they keep their voices down, don't spill cranberry juice on the modem, and do whatever it is they're supposed to be doing.

It's an ideal setup, actually.

* * *

The origin of today's home office is in the small family business. A while ago, the big-box stores—Best Buy, Office Depot, Staples, and others—woke up and realized that a dominant influencer of the contemporary home office culture was the female of the species. If you pay a visit to a Staples or Office Depot, it's striking to see how the stores have de-industrialized themselves in favor of something softer and even more whimsical. Where there used to be reams of computer paper and an assortment of binders that ran the gamut from black to white, there is now a wall of multicolored binders, from red to aquamarine, as well as another wall offering mix-and-match stationery. Purple and orange and yellow envelopes mixed with green or red writing paper.

The printing paper is still there, of course. The section simply acknowledges the female consumer, that's all.

Another new touch Office Max has introduced is an office-supply bubble gum machine of sorts, where for $9.99 a pound, a female consumer can buy stylish paper clips in fun shapes, push pins, and colored binder clips, weigh her purchase, then tote it to the register. Think salad bar, but instead of kalamata olives and mozzarella balls, females can pick out an assortment of playful office supplies that go beyond the merely functional. For Office Max, the margin on these items is substantial. To the male of the species, these doodads may seem unnecessary, but for the female, there's an operational incentive: perhaps she's thinking about creative, imaginative ways to manage paper, and about color as a tool to be able to communicate something essential about herself, and about the culture of her home environment.

Does this mean men are indifferent to color? No—just that today's office supply stores have recognized that there's a substantial feminine ethos in the creation of a home office, whether it's the binders on the wall, or the artificial palm plants that Staples now sells that lend animation to a workplace, or the fact that Staples.com allows customers to buy candy year-round, from Reese's

Pieces to Twizzlers—a very popular perk, I might add, in Envirosell's own New York office. And if it's candy you want, it can be no coincidence that Godiva chocolate is for sale just a few feet away from Staples' in-house SWAT team, Easy Tech.

That said, for the working woman, the home office often functions as a secondary seat of command. Though the kitchen may be the de facto social center of the house, within the home office reside the glowing motor, cords, Ethernet cables, installation manuals, and to-do calendars of what keeps that kitchen, not to mention the rest of the house and the life of her family, operating efficiently. As far as her daily office life is concerned, the female head of the house can upload files or documents from work and catch up on any urgent e-mails that may have come in late. While files dot her workplace computer, she also keeps duplicates on her home system. In essence, she can engage efficiently with her work from the comfort of her home, while at the same time keeping tabs on what's going on in her domestic life.

Why? Because the contemporary home office often serves double duty as the family's "tech room," a place devoted not just to work, but to a female's home-slash-family responsibilities. Anyone is welcome—and that means you, too, children! As far as her family is concerned, a female can make sure that the little ones have uploaded their homework from their schools' websites, and are getting underway on that endangered species report, or the French conjugations worksheet. Because everyone is crowded in the same physical space, busy typing away on his or her own laptop, a woman can make sure everybody is doing what they are supposed to be doing. Meanwhile, the female of the household can tackle her own work, return e-mails, use Epicurious.com to hunt down a recipe for horseradish mashed potatoes, order a book from Amazon, or if she's curious and confident enough to have created her own Facebook account (somehow she overruled her children, who voted against the idea as unseemly), she can digitally socialize with old classmates and other people she's lost touch with.

Thanks to the women who've driven product development at

Hewlett-Packard over the past decade, we've seen the introduction of what in industry parlance is known as MOPY. The acronym stands for Multiple Original Prints + Y. In other words, "Why Copy When You Can MOPY?" It's better known as the all-in-one printer. Built into this deluxe contraption is an incoming and outgoing fax machine, a scanner to replicate old photos and files or else turn them into digital documents, and a copier, which works on both black-and-white and color documents. Of course, there's a printer, too. Females are often the de facto custodians of their families' histories. With a MOPY, they can use a few megabytes of memory to upload digitalized photos of birthdays, anniversaries, and vacations, save them onto a blank CD, tuck the thing into a sleeve, label it, and catalogue it in a drawer by name and date. No more boxfuls of curling photos and old Polaroids.

Thanks to its versatility, the MOPY is a terrific time cruncher. Again, it extends the idea of importing what once usually involved a handful of errands (copying important papers, faxing something from Staples, developing photos at Walgreens) onto a single machine within the home environment. Even better, there's only a single plug involved.

Which means that at the end of the evening, the female of the house can print out, scan, copy, and fax everybody's stuff, from polar bear reports to French verb worksheets to spreadsheets.

Whether we find the notion appealing or appalling, a fail-safe way to lure twenty-first-century children into a room is via technology—a large-screen TV, a computer, a Wii. The screens are luminous. They ignite, entice, and give comfort the way fireplaces do. Even though sitting in front of a heated hearth may provide physical happiness, it doesn't give off the same promise of human connection that a Facebook account does. That's a different kind of warmth. In fundamental ways, both WiFi and wireless Bluetooth technology have made the home office possible. They've also wildly extended its physical boundaries. Today, the home office can migrate to a bedroom, a dining room, or a kitchen table. Yes, wiring up a house or apartment may require a computer with a centralized modem and router, but WiFi technology has freed all of us from having to sit at our desks on high-backed chairs. Instead, we can tote our laptop and cords and surf or toil on a futon, a basement couch, even in a hammock 150 yards from our houses and apartments.

As a resident of a densely populated city, whenever I log onto my own home network, I'm always surprised by the long list of WiFi'd people within just a single block radius. My neighbors' accounts have names like "The Reese Family" or "Jones/Merrill" or "Sparky the Dog." Each demands a secret codeword. My WiFi has a secret codeword, too, and well, sorry, I'm as territorial about my airspace as the next guy.

Whether she has a full-time or part-time job, or whether she's a working mother or both, the home office and the computer also functions as a place where the contemporary woman can surf the Internet to her heart's content. She can migrate from website to website, just looking, thank you, with no one the wiser and no commitments necessary. She (or for that matter, he) can catch up on the breaking news from CNN or the Huffington Post or the UK *Guardian* or *Le Figaro*. She can check out the latest fashions and bargains at Target or J.Crew or Pottery Barn or begin mulling over what her husband would like for his fiftieth birthday, or hunt down a cork bulletin board for her teenager's bedroom wall. She can preshop, i.e., research a product online so that when she finally comes face-to-face with an actual salesperson, she can proceed confidently forward with facts, figures, specs, and comps.

Thus, almost by chance, the Internet turns into a seminal resource for actual bricks-and-mortar retail environments. If she's at home or simply not feeling up to the task, a female interested in buying a new mobile phone or a refrigerator can research her purchase online by checking out a few consumer reports, then drive straight to the nearest Best Buy or Sears and buy the thing.

At Envirosell, we've found there to be an element of what we dub "secondary shopping therapy" for the female Internet user. Even if she lives in a small hamlet far from some cutting-edge urban metropolis, a woman can window-shop the best of what's happening in New York City or Los Angeles or Dublin or Tokyo, all via her Web browser. It's like strolling through some fabulous, animated women's magazine. She can gawk at stores and hotels and vacations, many of which may fall beyond her price range, and feel none the guiltier for it, or spied on, or self-conscious, or in any way implicated.

I've done some research on what makes a website appealing to females. For one, it has to have some entertainment value. It should also acknowledge what the purpose of being there is in the first place. Is it designed for the first-time visitor, or the repeat browser? How do Web designers make a Web presence a daily ritual, a pleasure, an up-to-the-moment indulgence, or a place of escape? What sets it apart from the zillions of other Internet sites out there?

From the standpoint of Web design, ongoing maintenance goes a long way, too. Recently I found myself on a website devoted to raising chickens (don't ask). It was last updated years ago. It felt moldy and suspect, and I moved along quickly.

Another element common to female-friendly websites is the creation of an environment—the digital equivalent of a furnished or wallpapered room. Amazon does this nicely, with its ever-changing lists and its many suggestions based on my previous spending habits. The site and I know and like each other and we can make a beeline. Also in terms of Web design appealing to women, colors and interesting shapes go a long way. Far too many websites are driven by masculine right angles. A computer itself is of course a rectangle—basically a box. When you think about it, mightn't a curved loggia or a gently sloping digital archway shake things up a little?

If you're after a female-unfriendly website, check out the Web presences of some of the office product superstores. Talk about bone-dry. They're like tool catalogues—their straightforwardness is their own worst enemy. Hotel.com and Travelocity are so business-focused they forget all about romancing the casual Internet browser. Another issue: If a female customer has to enter in too much information—or when it borders on the nosy, or intrusive—it becomes far easier for her to drop out. As I said, far more than males, women are conscious of their own personal safety. And a site that requests too much information too soon is like being chatted up by a creep.

Another critical element of the female home Internet browser has to do, again, with time-and-errand savings. She can use her home office's Internet connection to shop, thereby saving both money and more than one extra trip. Christmas and birthdays? Simply add to cart, click, and send. By avoiding the snaking lines that can deflate anyone's seasonal merriment, she can keep the spirit of the holiday alive without ever having to leave her own driveway. While she's at it, if she's an early-to-mid baby boomer, she can ponder whether an e-mailed thank-you note is acceptable from an etiquette point of view, or whether she should take the time to write a thank-you note the old-fashioned way (according to my contemporary protocol experts, an e-mailed thank-you note, while not as white-glove as pen to paper, is totally okay). She can also start figuring out ways to unload the heavy Oriental rugs and three banjo clocks she knows she'll inherit someday, but has no room for in her ultramodern, two-bedroom apartment.

If the contemporary female owns an old-fashioned filing cabinet, it will mostly be a repository of stuff she's printed out from her computer and MOPY. In this respect, the computer serves as a middleman—a cruncher and condenser of the extraneous data that floods her life and mailbox.

Finally? What if she doesn't want to watch *School of Rock* with her husband and children for the twelfth time? What if she's had it up to here with *The Princess Diaries 2*? While the rest of the family is watching Jack Black and Anne Hathaway doing their thing, the female of the house can retire to her home office and slip into the DVD slot of her desktop computer the first disc of the old Granada TV production of *Brideshead Revisited,* or season five of *House* that she downloaded from iTunes without telling anyone.

It's what her parents must have experienced thirty years earlier when they closed their own office doors. Solitude within reach of company, to paraphrase Saul Bellow. In other words, happiness.

5

WE CAN WORK IT OUT

We're at our local athletic club. Not to work out, mind you, just to observe.

We're stealing a few minutes from our day to observe the modern-day middle-age male. He's one of the few guys out there over a certain age who cares about the maintenance of his physical self. He doesn't live on either coast, so Looking Good is reserved for occasions that take place locally and in public at most twice a year. Today he's working the exercise bike and the Nautilus circuit inside a stadium-size room surrounded by walls of mirrors and cutting-edge machines that resemble a series of polished, oversize mollusks. Whatever direction he faces, the room reflects back at him, including a wall of eight TV sets broadcasting everything from soap operas to CNN to an *E! True Hollywood Story* about rock star wives.

Our guy is pushing fifty. His body is starting to show evidence of what happens to all male torsos, regardless of whether they take the stairs two at a time or the escalator. He's flaring out at the waist—"love handles" is the endearing euphemism. He's developing a gut. His butt is heading south. His breasts are getting puffy and tender. He has bags under his eyes and crinkles and moles everywhere else. It bugs him that attractive females no longer eyeball him when he walks along the sidewalk. Even bank tellers don't flirt with him anymore—another good reason to use the ATM. Thank God for the eminently accepting and loving woman in his life.

But he's determined to fight back. Hence the decision to sign up for a gym membership. At home, he still keeps an ancient weight stand in the basement, along with a few free weights of varying sizes and poundage, but his teenage son and his friends have co-opted his equipment, so our middle-aged man is reduced to going to the gym whenever he can spare an hour or so.

Still, when his year-long membership runs out, he forgets to renew. He won't go back to a gym for another five years, when his internist announces he'll no longer treat him unless he starts working out for twenty minutes regularly—walking, running, anything at all—three times a week.

At which point, his eyes zero in on the treadmill in his basement his wife bought years earlier and uses three or four times a week. When she bought it, it felt like a waste of money. Now he wonders what she knew all along that he didn't. His wife agrees to let him use it if he sprays it down when he's done.

Whether they're serious female weight lifters, committed sportswomen, or simply want to keep in shape, females make heavy use of public gyms. The problem is, gyms can be visually, emotionally, and physically overstimulating—all those sharp angles, hard surfaces, and Spandexed bodies pumping and jerking and displaying, not to mention the sheer tonnage of the equipment. Fortunately for both genders, the contemporary gym has become all about multitasking. Not only is there that stall of overhead TVs, but the most desirable treadmills have small television screens built right into them. Attired with headphones, you can jog in place while watching Regis and Kelly, the local news, a home improvement show, or a rerun of last night's *Jon Stewart.* You can use the Stairmaster while listening to a Podcast interview with the Dalai Lama, or an NPR interview with Bono you somehow missed during your work commute. Some aerobics machines even have dedicated shelves for reading books or magazines.

Maybe the athletic club brought in all this gadgetry when it realized it had a serious competitor in the home gym. Because if there's enough space, many females have dedicated a room in their own house to—well—"wellness" is the term that seems to be in vogue these days.

I'm not mocking the word. For many females, concepts like "wellness" and "balance" have much to do with resolving their uncertain relationship with themselves, and in some cases serving to remind themselves they even have one, i.e., "Where did I go?" Women fulfill a multitude of roles across all societies. They're wives, mothers, professionals, and as daughters, the point persons for aging parents. The concept of a woman taking ninety minutes to tend to herself is a far more natural assumption than it is for a man. After all, a great many people depend on her. And if she has children, certainly there is some holdover from the physical phenomenon of pregnancy and childbirth—namely, if she doesn't tend to herself, she can't be as available to all the people in her life.

According to a report issued by the Bureau of Labor Statistics, across the United States, men and women with high levels of education are far more likely to participate in sports or any kind of recreation. Just getting a college degree makes someone twice as likely to participate in a sport. Since we know what gender is dominating higher education right now and will be in the decades to come, it makes sense.

For women, the home gym has everything to do with being present, available, and in control while simultaneously doing something beneficial for themselves. It has to do with maintaining mastery over the household without that pinch of guilt that nags at many females, namely, that if they devote time to themselves that doesn't promote the well-being of their families, then either they're shirking or being selfish. Accordingly, the home gym allows for the encapsulation and multitasking of a finite amount of time within a female's busy schedule. Taking an hour to work up a sweat on the Stairmaster, run in place, or pedal on an Exercycle, then follow it up with a few dips, bends, sit-ups, yoga stretches, and free weights, is a great way to keep an eye on the big picture while tending to one's own health and sanity.

Also according to the Bureau of Labor Statistics, women are also more likely to engage in sports and exercise with other family members, while men work out with friends (for males, this is a way of banishing social awkwardness through triangulating). The invention of the single or double jogging stroller where a new mother can get in her miles while the baby reclines and sleeps probably kicked off this trend—a rising heart rate for a new mom trying to get back into prepregnancy shape, fresh air, and a bizarre experience for Baby.

At some juncture in most men's lives, vanity takes a backseat. Preoccupation with his physical self is seen as fussy, preening, and unmanly. Past the mating stage, it's something a male is expected to outgrow. In his late forties and fifties, the typical male allows his body to morph into a no-frills transportation device. In those decades, a male is traditionally evaluated by his professional success and his ability to provide for his family. Male menopause may be real, but it's subtle. For women, the awareness of change, physically and hormonally, is striking. For females who are more invested than men are in looking as good as possible, and for longer, too, exercising is an essential ingredient of leading a sane life.

Again, infomercials targeting women have certainly played a part in this home workout environment. Ads for home exercise equipment devote little time to the science or aerodynamics of whatever miracle device is being hawked—that's guy stuff—but instead focus on how a female can flatten her abs or tighten her tummy or shrink her hips in only twenty minutes, two or three times a week. The Bowflex may sell well to males, but what sells in spectacular numbers to females are gadgets such as the Ab Roller.

Picture it: A woman stretches on the floor over this strange rocking apparatus, seizes the handles, and commences a forward-and-backward rocking motion. Ten minutes later, she can swear her abs are tighter, but even better, ten minutes is just that, ten minutes—which frees her up to attend to the rest of her life.

Many home exercise rooms women have put together feature an area devoted to hushed contemplation—a yoga or Pilates mat, a scented candle, a pair of iPod speakers with an exercise playlist, even a small television set linked to a DVD machine, where a woman who's risen early and downed a cup of coffee can replicate the moves of a male or female exercise instructor against a beautiful backdrop, usually Hawaiian.

Yoga is 26,000 years old. It has its roots as a male discipline and was first practiced by men in the caves of India. The word itself derives from the Sanskrit word, "yuj," which means to join or unite, in this case with a universal spirit. Today, though, go to any yoga studio and the class in session will be comprised of approximately 90 percent women. Time constraints, as well as the overwhelming whiff of the feminine, are probably what discourages most men from practicing yoga. It's gentle. It's inward-looking. It's antiperfectionism. It's noncompetitive—at least overtly. My yoga-devoted friends swear it instills in them a balance that's both external and internal, one that takes them through the day.

The only exceptions to the female dominance of yoga are hybrid forms of the discipline such as Bikram yoga, which takes place in a studio heated to a hundred degrees, and has more in common with marine boot camp at Parris Island than with yoga. The only thing missing are the sand fleas. The body sweats out roughly 750 calories as a no-nonsense instructor barks out orders through a miked headphone. The moans, groans, and sighs you hear around you are animalistic, almost sexual in nature. Bikram practitioners have been known to get light-headed, to throw up, and get nosebleeds. They're encouraged to work through their discomfort. No wonder it attracts a squadron of modern male gladiators. But there are a whole lot of female Bikram warriors, too.

Think about it, though—in a home gym, there's no membership fee, no other people, no one watching, a routine can last as long as you like, and the only waiting list involves the female of the house deciding whether or not she wants to work out today or not, and if so, whether she does so in the morning or at night.

We've entered an era where females have embraced what you might term "soulful exercise." No jolting or pounding of the knees. No ten-mile bike rides or eight-mile uphill runs. Instead, Pilates, yoga, and active walking, maybe with an iPod and an actress reading from the latest Eckhart Tolle or Sue Grafton book, or maybe even James Earl Jones booming out the King James Bible. It beats driving over to the gym, changing into gym clothes, snatching a rushed Stairmaster experience, avoiding the ogles of strange males, showering in an unclean stall, suiting up in your civilian clothes, and either going to work or going back home—which, depending on what time it is, can turn what was originally intended to bring a female health, equanimity, and rejuvenation into a frazzling, unpleasant, two-hour hole cut out of her day.

Recognizing this, more and more athletic clubs have accommodated themselves to the needs of today's time-starved female, including the Curves chain, which promises the equivalent of a ninety-minute workout in a half-hour circuit workout. It has four million female members. It's even launched a line of granola bars and popcorn, vitamins, tank tops, and capri pants. In most modern gyms, the days are gone when the only person who could show you how to use the lat pulldown or triceps extension was some slick, overly tanned gym professional. Today at most athletic clubs, there are as many female trainers as men. And just as the modern-day supermarket now offers an in-store Boston Market or Dunkin' Donuts to compete with a consumer's fast-food dollar, many gyms now feature their own yoga, Pilates, and rock-climbing classes, as well as masseuses, to rival stand-alone studios. Some clubs have opened up cafes, too, where after working out, a pair of female friends can sit down for a liter of sparkling designer water, or using the club's WiFi, check the latest headlines from CNN.

The cafe offers a selection of such fare as whole-grain muffins and turkey-and-alfalfa sprout sandwiches.

That said, if a female has her own home workout room, and the desire and money to hire a personal trainer, or a yoga or Pilates instructor who makes house calls, it's far easier to maintain a personal relationship in your own home than it could ever be in a cavernous, overpopulated, multimirrored public arena replete with sign-up sheets for the best machines. Going to a gym doesn't just take time out of your day. It's a solitary experience carried out in public. It's an internal conversation between you and a row of impersonal machines, whereas an in-home personal trainer can both individualize and perpetuate a female's own self-image. Even better, the female doesn't have to commute, which is no small issue, especially in densely populated urban areas. A home gym also puts to rest issues of vanity and appearance. At home, there aren't seventy-five people staring at her as she works the ab machine, only a single trainer-cheerleader. It's always easier to attain your exercise goals when another person is encouraging you to do your best.

A home gym is all about a dedication to an ideal, rather than a woman having to confront the issue of dedication itself. Whether or not a female opts to create a room of her own, the home exercise nook is one created with her in mind.

6

TO LOVE, HONOR, AND MAINTAIN

I spent my childhood and early adolescence overseas. My father was in the diplomatic service, and we spent time in Indonesia, Malaya, the Philippines, Korea, and briefly, Poland, before returning to the States. Except for two years in Warsaw, where my parents employed a single employee who was responsible for cleaning and food preparation, we had multiple servants throughout my childhood. In Malaya, we had a cook, an upstairs maid, and two gardeners. In Korea, we had a cook, an upstairs and a downstairs maid, a houseboy, two gardeners, and a driver. We weren't being fancy—they came with the job. Throughout much of the Far East, even modest middle-income families generally have a live-in staff of some kind. I have a good friend, José Luis Nueno, who lives by himself in an apartment in Barcelona. José Luis has two Filipina maids. One or the other is there on the premises twenty-four hours a day. They get paid a modest salary. No one blinks twice.

Whenever I'm visiting other parts of the world, particularly emerging markets, I'm reminded of the normalcy of a servant class.

If you're an upscale Brazilian family, for example, you probably live in a house teeming with hired hands who, in their spare time, sit in the kitchen paging through design and fashion magazines. In Brazil, the kitchen is where the servants hang out, as opposed to in America, where the kitchen is where family members come together to catch up on their day. Where are the live-in servants in America? They've mostly vanished from our landscape. With the exception of the ultrarich, most of us have reached a point where we do our own housework.

When Envirosell was doing our first work on consumers and vacuum cleaners, we conducted a study in a Walmart. We were looking at couples shopping for vacs. One thing we discovered was that males were very, and I mean *extremely,* interested in the horsepower of the machines they were looking at. They correlated "suck!" and "speed!" with power. Guys wanted a vacuum cleaner with a real Hummer engine to get the job done. One clear selling point, we informed the manufacturer, was to spell out the amperage of the machine right up front.

In my own apartment, I have three vacuum cleaners. One lives downstairs, one lives upstairs, and there's a mini in the kitchen to take care of quick messes. The ascendancy of the female in our culture means the rise not just of power, but of labor-saving devices, of which the best known today is probably the Swiffer cleaning cloth. Swiffer began its life as a dry cloth, migrated to a wet cloth, and now also comes in spray form. It's one of a new generation of household chemical delivery systems that are all about speed and efficiency, and are fundamentally anti-Green.

Thus, on one hand, we may have next-door neighbors who talk at length about reducing their carbon footprints, but when we sneak a peek into their kitchens, it's all Swiffer, all the time.

In Malaya, when I was in the fifth and sixth grades, my mother would reserve one day a week when we would send the servants home and pretend we were a real American family, the homegrown kind. My sister and I made our own beds, and my mother cooked breakfast, lunch, and dinner, U.S.A.-style. Having grown up in a family of some means, my mother's cooking skills were minimal—grilled cheese sandwiches mostly. It must have come as a small relief to her when our American family days came to an end.

When we moved back to the States, to Chevy Chase, Maryland, a maid came in once a week. My mother did a limited share of the family laundry. I was sent away to school in New England, where as a boarder, along with the other boys, we had to keep our rooms clean and sweep and make our beds. It was away from home that I first acquired the skill of using a washing machine and dryer. I enjoyed it, too.

In my own home, I'm extremely conscious of the evolution of grooming products. Over the course of my life as a male, I've observed and sometimes used distinct innovations—from the blue blade to the stainless-steel blade to the injector razor to the double blade with the sensor strip to the Quattro. The styptic pencil—remember that thing? I haven't owned or even seen one of those in probably twenty-five years. Men just don't cut themselves shaving anymore, at least not the way we used to, wads of tissue on our necks and chins.

The same goes for cleaning products. The Swiffer represents a massive step forward, effectively replacing, and improving on, the mop. It feels—there's the word again—*cleaner*. Its movable head goes places traditional mops can't. You're not dealing with squeezed-out and occasionally dirty water. Once a Swiffer head turns gray, it's easy to replace the thing. As we like to say at Envirosell, women don't end at the appliance—they turn technology into appliances because they're interested not in what it does, but a) how it does it; and b) how it will enhance and enrich their lives.

But that's just basic cleaning. Thanks to women, the maintenance of the house has gotten a whole lot more mechanical—and female.

·

Remember the little neighborhood kid with the snow shovel?

We'll call him Bobby. He was as much an American wintertime archetype as mistletoe. At the first sign of a snowstorm, and assuming the town had canceled school that day, the doorbell would ring and there he'd be, all zippered up and wet-mittened, offering to clear your walkway, swipe away stray icicles, and shovel out your car. For five or ten bucks, of course.

Most people (except those with indolent teenage sons sleeping in) were happy to open their wallets for a good cause.

I don't know about you, but Bobby hasn't shown up at my door in about a decade, and that's not because there haven't been any blizzards, or because I live in New York City, and the snow rarely stays for long. My friends in the suburbs and exurbs say the same thing—Bobby is gone.

These days, the person shoveling and sanding your front steps is probably an extremely resourceful female, and—oh—she might very well share your living quarters.

Wait, though, why is this? This isn't some atavistic return to the female doing even more than she usually does around the house, is it? No, Bobby's departure forms a backdrop to something more integral to the larger culture.

First off, menial labor such as shoveling driveways is something at which, over the past few years, a lot of American kids have turned up their noses. In a lot of summer resort towns, companies ship in hundreds of immigrant kids to work jobs as ice-cream scoopers, chambermaids, and hostess/servers that many native-born teenagers won't touch. One summer it will be Brazilians, the next Ukrainians, the following year a crowd of smiling, freckled Irish kids streaming across Nantucket, Martha's Vineyard, Cape Cod, and the Hamptons. These good souls are not averse to sharing cheap lodging, making and saving money, and for those who spent their childhoods in countries that rarely saw the sun, bringing home a great tan when Labor Day rolls around.

Who's left, then? The man of the house, if there is one. But what if he's the sole breadwinner, and is in his car heading to work by seven in the morning? We're left with the female, who's not content merely to oversee her family's schedule but in some cases to literally redefine the role of homemaker—as the maker (and preserver) of the home, both its interior and exterior.

The tool-belt diva is a female, who in some cases can caulk and seal, retile the tub, replace the bath fan and light, fiddle with the garage door opener so it works, install track lighting, build a bi-fold door, custom shelving, and a skylight, and you should see her with a paintbrush, too . . .

If she's in her forties now, her skills may have been shaped by simple generational exigencies. Maybe she's a product of divorce and grew up with a single mother. Maybe she was always a person interested in taking things apart and learning how they worked. A lot of female teens in the 1970s and '80s found they had an aptitude for this kind of work by taking an active role behind the scenes in high school theater productions. It was satisfying, good for their self-esteem, and also gave them a crash course in painting, lighting, and design. Plus, in those days, as mothers kept reminding daughters, anything a boy could do, a girl could do as well. So in some respects, the era permitted and even pushed a generation of young women toward mechanical self-sufficiency.

If that didn't do the trick, graduating from college did. As they were getting their feet wet in the job market, many young women lived alone, or shared an apartment with a female roommate. Even if they had men in their lives, these women weren't about to play the role of Helpless Female. They were typically on a budget, too, which left them one choice: *Figure it out.* Overhead lights not working? Measure and replace the tubes. Paint peeling? Prime and repaint the wall. Kitchen faucet spraying uncontrollably? Replace the washer. Either that, or shell out seventy-five bucks minimum to some strange guy who'll fix whatever's not working, and that's assuming you can find someone available *and* you felt secure enough to allow an unfamiliar male with a box of tools over your all-female threshold.

I know a forty-eight-year-old woman who's an absolute whiz at home repair. She told me about her "eureka!" moment, which took place when she was in her midteens and living with her mother and sister. One month, she noticed that it was taking longer and longer to dry recently washed clothes and there was an acrid smell coming from the basement. As a person who liked taking things apart and seeing how they worked, she poked around the dryer only to come upon what she later learned was commonly called a "lint trap." It was so overheated, so encrusted with fuzz and gunk, that the plastic had started to burn.

"I remember it so clearly because with one swipe of my hand, I fixed this big alien machine, maybe saved us all from a house fire, and eliminated the need to call a repair man. Oh, and don't even get me started on living without our little black-and-white TV when Mom took it to the repair shop to replace the plug my older sister had cut off because she thought I was watching too much television. I cried for a week. Do you know how *easy* it is to replace a plug?"

Today, the Internet devotes millions of Web pages to home repair—everything from replacing exterior light fixtures to finessing bathroom duct work to adding a shower to your bathtub to insulating an attic to refacing and refinishing your kitchen cabinets. Home repair isn't for everybody. A female has to find stuff like this interesting and challenging; she has to have an aptitude for it; and as in my friend's case, she has to be a little, well, *tight*. For many women, homemaking has taken on broader parameters than keeping the children healthy and dressed, setting a nice Sunday table, and juggling multiple schedules. It includes the responsibility of economizing the household. For many homemakers, toolbelt diva is simply part of the job description. Homemaking isn't only keeping a house clean and beautiful; it's also addressing (and budgeting for) those cracks and peels that keep it from looking clean and beautiful.

From Julia Child to Martha Stewart, the past several decades have exposed American females to a guilt-inducing gallery of "We can do it, so why can't you?" superwomen. Not to mention countless cable TV home-improvement channel networks (one, HGTV, airs approximately seventy-seven different home-renovation programs every week or month). Just as the birth of the department store in the 1860s exposed a typical middle-class person to a selection of goods and services she could aspire to, these TV shows, which are both addicting and narratively satisfying, have exposed a generation of women to what they can do, if they're so inclined, to their dwellings. However, unlike the department store, it's not about things, but projects.

And if she doesn't want to spend time watching these TV shows, the contemporary female can log onto a website like Be Jane, which targets female do-it-yourselfers. Women, after all, spend roughly $50 billion in the home improvement industry every year. The point of Be Jane is for women to wrest control of the home environment back from the historically male-dominated home improvement market, so females can implement these changes themselves, without calling in a grizzled, chain-smoking, occasionally nervous-making SWAT team of carpenters and contractors. This same trend of do-it-yourselfism dovetails with the rebirth of the craft moment, whether it's homemade soap making, knitting, or quilting. The crafting of photo albums and scrapbooking—traditionally female ways to curate and catalogue the life and times of their families—are making big comebacks.

For a time, big box home stores tried to target the female handywoman, but these chains quickly lost ground. The original demographic was professional contractors, and these stores' attempts to widen their circle of customers was a mixed success. By opening their doors to noncontractors, some lost more than a few members of their original customer base.

I had an interesting moment once at Lowe's where a group of ten managers took me inside a prototype store. Only one of them was female. "I'd like to go see a women's bathroom," I said. Once the coast was clear, we walked in. The bathroom was clean and white, kind of plain Jane. I went over to one of the walls and knocked. "What's on the other side of the wall?" I asked one of the group. "That's where we keep bathroom fashion," he said. "Hmm, why isn't it in here?" I said. It felt like a winning idea to me. Why couldn't you get Kohler, say, and maybe a couple of other bathroom and fixture designers, to install toilets and sinks in the women's restroom? If a significant number of women use this room, wouldn't it be a great opportunity to create some buzz, for female consumers to see how actual products for sale worked in real life? If you think about every major new hotel or restaurant across our larger landscape, you realize that having a fantastic women's bathroom is a design statement that creates buzz. If you have any doubt, check out the women's bathroom at the Delano Hotel in Miami's South Beach. It's out of this world.

But back to my tool-belt diva friend. The only time she'll take a step back and cede control to a professional is when there's too much muscle involved—ladders and such—or when the costs of the tools involved overwhelm the actual project (does any female—or for that matter, male—really want to buy a ten-inch double-bevel sliding compound miter saw to carry out a half-hour job?).

Another element driving many tool-belt divas is a new perspective: the home as an art project. Men, they say, paint the house when it needs it; women paint the house when they get bored with the color. The act of being tool-belt Jane has a stronger relationship to craft than it does to an actual occupation. Beginning when he was a boy, with those noisy, clattering Lincoln Logs, the male tool-belt guy is all about building, whereas for Jane, there's often a form of artistic satisfaction in her efforts.

To me, one of the most interesting "Aha!" moments is realizing that men are letting women play with power tools. My dad had always built stuff—furniture, sofas, even the bed I slept in—though I was never allowed inside his rec shop. For years I heard him banging away at some piece of furniture or another, generating clouds of dust. It was a constant source of family amusement that my father, Francis, was more dedicated to woodworking than he was actually good at it.

A seminal moment in my own family came about when my father announced his retirement. A short time later my mother began taking a carpentry course, and only a few months after that, she built a Shaker dry sink that today sits in my downstairs guest room. I'm not sure if my father ever forgave her. How had she just strolled in there and made something so beautiful while he was spending his off-work hours making cabinets that, for whatever reason, never came out right? It's no surprise that my dad's rec shop became known as the Pout House.

Speaking of fathers, where do guys fit into this new environment of the tool-belt diva? In many cases, men are grateful and relieved, rather than resentful. For whatever reasons, most guys aren't being taught this kind of fix-it stuff anymore. Maybe they never learned it from their own fathers. As for other family members who might have taught the kid how to grout tile, well, in today's mobile society, they all live so far away from one another it's not as though you can call up your handyman uncle at a moment's notice.

Incidentally, my tool-belt diva acquaintance is married to an international businessguy who's hopeless with home repair. He's not embarrassed—it's just not his thing. Not knowing what to do with Sheetrock or how to fix a clogged toilet represents no affront whatsoever to his manhood. He has great admiration for his wife's talents, and as a consultant who charges by the hour and travels a lot, he appreciates that her efforts save their family money. At this point in his life, it makes little economic sense for a man who's earning a good hourly wage to devote those same hours to figuring out the difference between a regular and a Phillips head screwdriver. He's more than happy to cede the fix-it part of being the Man of the House to his far more capable wife.

My friend has a very bright ten-year-old daughter. Her mother is teaching her some of the tricks of the trade. Sometimes her daughter shows an interest, sometimes not. But what her mother wants—"and it may just be my issue," she adds—"is for her never to play the helpless female."

7

SHOULD I STAY OR SHOULD I GO?

Good afternoon, Mr. Underhill! Checking in to our hotel? *Fantastic!* And how will you be paying today, Mr. Underhill? *Fantastic!* Oh, and Mr. Underhill, we hope you'll take advantage of our restaurant, Rafters, which serves up Polynesian-fusion cuisine, including our signature Twelve-Spice Duck on a Dune of Caramelized Lingonberry Mâché . . .

All right, I get the picture.

I don't mind hearing my name spoken aloud in a crowded hotel lobby, but put yourself for a moment in the shoes of a jet-lagged female traveler. She's tired, thirsty, and for the past several hours, she's been fantasizing about those crisp, white sheets awaiting her once her plane touched down. Right this instant, she wants nothing more than to check into her hotel room with no fuss and no attention, other than the polite, efficient kind.

Think about it. Does she, or for that matter any female, *really* want to hear her name called out two or three times by some well-intentioned but unthinking hotel employee? Does she *really* want everybody in the lobby, including that weedy fellow in the corner reading the *X-Men* comic book, to know she's traveling solo?

What men want and women look for in a hotel experience is a traveling snapshot of what men and women care about in their everyday lives. If most males are indifferent to a little grime and disorder around the far borders of the places they live, eat, and sleep, most women aren't. Guys may not care about bathroom lighting, or mirrors, or what amenities crowd the little blond wicker basket atop the toilet, or whether only a single locked double door separates the room from that of the person or couple next door, but most women do. The only thing males may notice about the hair dryer in the hotel bathroom are the aeronautics involved in how the designer got the thing to adhere to the wall just so, but the average female traveler may take note of its make, voltage, and also how far its cord extends. While she's at it, she'll also note the room's cleanliness, lighting, temperature, color (or lack thereof), flooring, the size, shape, and firmness of the pillows on the bed, and whether or not she feels safe—emotionally, physically, psychologically—and at home. She'll do this unconsciously, too. One thumb-smudged remote control, one rogue hair in the bathroom sink, and the front desk will probably be hearing from her.

Women *notice* this stuff. And many hotels, at least the smart ones, have recognized the power of the female, and are responding.

My paternal grandfather ran a wholesale dairy business out of New York City. He traveled and bought and brought back butter, eggs, and milk from as far west as Montana. He liked to tell Dutchman jokes, though being a kindly and honorable man, I'm fairly sure he chose the Dutch as the safest, least controversial targets of his humor. Most of these tales involved Dutchmen who wandered into hotels, aka, "So this Dutchman walked into a hotel in Kansas City . . ." The rest is unprintable.

The point is, commercial traveling has historically been a solitary male profession. Until at least the 1960s, a working woman who drifted from city to city without a husband or male companion was generally perceived as a member of some frowned-upon, usually suspect profession.

Since the beginning of time, human beings have wandered, and required places to sleep other than their own beds. In ancient times, Greece had its resorts and mineral and hot springs, England had its inns, and the Middle East had both its caravansaries and its khans. In the Middle Ages, monasteries and abbeys offered shelter to travelers, as did certain hospitaliers, who offered asylum for Crusaders and pilgrims as they rode or trudged their way to the Holy Land.

Still, can it be any coincidence that the most mobile, restless country in the world—the United States—should have given birth to the world's first hotels? The rapid-fire urbanization of the eighteenth, nineteenth, and twentieth centuries depended on Americans' ability to move around the country at will and rest their heads somewhere at night. In the United States, hotels began their lives as public houses. These were fleabag joints that sold hooch and could host a traveler in a bed he'd often be obliged to share with a gin-soaked stranger and a bedbug or two. These public houses multiplied in the early 1800s, as the prevalence of oceangoing trade and transatlantic shipping necessitated the need for places where a merchant and his crew could rest their tired bodies.

The first hotels were private homes opened to the public by entrepreneurial women, usually widows hoping to make a little extra cash. Struggling families rented out other family's attics or basements. The middle class took in boarders or else moved into other people's dwellings. The hotel evolved from being a single-family dwelling into a boardinghouse into an apartment building that, by the middle of the nineteenth century, housed a truly remarkable number of Americans. In the middle of the nineteenth century, by one estimate, nearly three quarters of middle- and upper-class New Yorkers lived in a hotel or a boardinghouse.

The expansion of the American railroads coincided with the construction of the very first real hotels, whose popularity coincided with the first stirrings of the emancipation of American women. In those days, the division of economic labor was simple. Men worked, often away from home, in factories and firms. Women stayed at home, cooking, cleaning, sewing, washing, drying, tending to the children, and keeping an eye on the clock, waiting for their husbands to come home. Imagine the profound sense of liberation that the first hotels offered the housebound, put-upon female since, by then, the rise of higher-paying factory jobs had all but eliminated the servant class. With in-house cooking staffs, kitchens, chambermaids, and on-site laundresses, the hotel subverted the traditional, gendered order of labor. Many "progressive" families opted to raise their children in this revolutionary new environment, which relieved the female of the house from day-to-day drudgery, and left her time to raise and educate her children.

Critics at the time charged that this arrangement would do lasting damage to women, and to society as a whole. Some blamed hotels for playing havoc with traditional family life, and that females, freed from old-fashioned wifely duties, would become slothful. Early feminist writers responded that women had been subordinated for centuries, and that gender inequality was rooted in domestic life. After all, with their hands full of babies and dirty laundry, how could females possibly be expected to develop minds of their own?

My interest in hotels isn't merely historical or anecdotal. As someone who travels almost half the year, they play an important part of my life. Over the past two decades, I've stayed in hotels large and small, deluxe and not-so-deluxe, roadside joints that resemble minimum-security pens, and, back in the days when Envirosell was just starting out and I didn't know whether or not it would succeed as an ongoing business, a motel equipped with a steering wheel, wipers, automatic transmission, muffler, catalytic converter and at night, a driver's seat pressed backward into reclining position (yes, it was my car, and I'd shave, brush my teeth, and freshen up as needed inside the nearest gas station men's room).

I happen to take hotels very seriously, and not only because my

New York staff is made up of a large percentage of female employees whose comfort and peace of mind concern me, especially when we're working in cities or countries with dodgy reputations. We have a company-wide mandate that we don't ever send our employees, male or female, to any hotel where there's direct access to the rooms from a portal that's not the lobby. If you've ever taken a stroll around the outside of a motel, you know what I'm talking about—that single door near the spookily humming ice machine, the one that leads into a dimly lit parking lot. No thanks.

I have an unhappy story involving that particular motel back door (well, I have a few, but this one sticks in my craw). I was staying once at a Comfort Inn in Hendersonville, North Carolina. The chain's plainly stated pledge is "100 percent satisfaction guaranteed-or-else your visit is free." My first night there, I noticed that the outside door that opened out onto the parking lot was broken, and that the lock wouldn't fasten, no matter how many times I tried to manhandle it shut. Any vagrant or wanderer or worse could have snuck in through the parking lot, made his way upstairs and held up or assaulted some innocent traveler at gunpoint.

I was there for three nights. The day before I checked out, I brought up the busted back door issue with the general manager. "The lock doesn't work," I said. "Security is an important issue for a business traveler, and you didn't fulfill your promise." I wasn't trying to weasel out of paying my bill, but what about that Comfort Inn pledge of 100 percent customer satisfaction? In so many words, the manager told me to take a hike, and that if I was so unhappy, I should have switched motels after my first night. As a balm, Comfort Inn management offered me free breakfast my last day—a Styrofoam cup of coffee-colored hot water and a bagel so hard you could have skipped it across Loch Ness.

That was the last time I've stayed in a Comfort Inn.

Today, within the hierarchy of hotels, there's a clear-cut, ascending pyramid of trade. The budget motel category includes Motel 6, whereas the Comfort Inn chain sits squarely inside the economy channel. Next up is entry-level luxury, such as Hilton's Garden

Inn and the Marriott Courtyard. One step above entry-level luxury is the standard business hotel, the Marriotts and Hyatts, followed by the so-called representational business hotels, like the St. Regis and the Crowne Plaza. At the very top of the line, you have the luxury and über-luxury categories, and for the high roller who truly believes that what happens in Vegas stays in Vegas, the over-the-top glitzy casino hotels. Let's not overlook the family resorts, either, such as the Disney Cruise Lines—noisy, jovial places that go out of their way to appeal to children.

Every country has its own variations on the hotel. In Japan, where the population density is roughly ten times greater than it is in the United States, you'll find the phenomenon known as a capsule hotel. I've never stayed in one; I'm just too tall. But imagine you're a hard-working businessman who commutes to downtown Tokyo from some outlying burg. It's been a long day, it's late at night, and the last thing you feel like doing is boarding the train for the ride home. To the rescue comes the capsule hotel, where for approximately thirty-five bucks a night, you can slide yourself into a narrow sleeping compartment. You don't enter the capsule from the side or from the middle and sit down, or flop down, as you do with most beds; you go in from one end and kind of shimmy your way forward. The capsule hotel room is clean, private, no frills and if you're at all prone to claustrophobia or panic attacks, impossible even to imagine. Still, it has everything a tired body might need: a tiny TV bolted to the ceiling, an alarm clock, a small mirror, and a ventilation nozzle such as you find above your seat on airplanes. Some capsule rooms are stacked two-high. There could be a thousand in one building, with the men on one floor, the women on another.

Another concept that has yet to catch on in the States and most likely never will is the love hotel. Across South America, where grown children and their spouses often still share an apartment with their parents, love hotels, known colloquially as "telos," aren't just an indulgence, they're a necessity. Imagine that you're a Latino man or woman in an amorous mood. Sure, you can stretch out next to your loved one and start fooling around, but with Mom in the next room dicing vegetables for stew, and Dad watching the football game, it's not exactly an environment that encourages friskiness. Within this context, the love hotel, where you and your spouse can roll around for a few hours, allows you to enjoy a degree of sexual freedom that would be awkward in an apartment you share with your parents.

Regardless, somewhere along the line, hotels have redefined the way many of us offer up hospitality, home-style. My own basement guest room has a queen-size Murphy bed. When I'm putting someone up for the night, I lay out fresh towels and washcloths, and my guest bathroom is filled with countless doodads I've picked up from my travels, from body wash to thumb-size bottles of conditioner to minicontainers of shaving cream. There's a TV, an alarm clock, a sleep mask, three shelves' worth of bedtime reading, and I'll even give you my password if you brought along your laptop and want to surf the Web using the WiFi. While literally subterranean, my guest room is quiet, carpeted, and comfortable, it's what most guests expect, and I know their happiness level has more than a little to do with the fact that it partially mimics a standard hotel room.

We're at the front desk. Want to check in?

By 2010, it's safe to say that every major hotel chain in the world has rechoreographed hotels and hotel services with the single female traveler in mind. Recent innovations range from the bowed shower curtains and clotheslines over the bathtub to lighted closets to the redesign of those same closets—including the mix of hangers, from shirt to skirt, and the ability of those very same hangers to detach from the rod—considering that no guest, male or female, likes to feel that the hotel management has so little trust in him or her that anything that's not nailed down will be stolen—to today's obsession with pillows.

But the hotel experience begins when you first pass through the revolving doors and into the lobby.

A few years back, we did a job for the Starwood Group, studying one of its Sheraton hotels both before and after an extensive lobby renovation. Not surprisingly, we found that men make up a significant percentage of those who spend time in a lobby—what we at Envirosell dub "dwell time." Men tended to show up alone, too, rather than in pairs. Maybe they were after a change of scenery, or an opportunity to people watch, or they just wanted to stretch their legs and explore the confines of the building. In the lobby, single men typically took a seat where they took advantage of the free Wi-Fi and fiddled away with their BlackBerries and iPhones and laptops and spreadsheets. Or they were there to welcome a visitor—most of the time, in fact, that was what they were doing. With exceptions, women perceive hotel lobbies as utilitarian places to go during check-in and check-out.

As our leisure time has leaked into our professional lives, most lobbies now feature a business center. It's one intended to appeal to both genders. Typically it features a couple of fax machines, a few Ethernet cables, a few laser-jet printers, and a bunch of wall sockets to keep your laptop energized. Here, the manners of personal communication between the sexes diverge, and in some cases overlap. Consider the mobile phone, an accessory so ubiquitous we forget it's been in our hands for less than two decades. Where do men tend to use their mobile phones? Wherever they happen to be, including hotel lobbies, and if you don't like overhearing them touch base with Scott or Jay in the home office, well, wear earplugs. The female of the species, however, with a touch more politesse, tends to gravitate to the edges of the lobby to conduct her conversations.

As guests arrive, practically all counters today now offer a raised marble check-in ledge, six to eight inches below the actual counter, where a female traveler can park her purse or briefcase. Increasingly, as I said, today's hotel staffers are trained to refrain from announcing the names of their guests or their room numbers. Instead, a clerk now steps out from behind the counter and presses the key, or an anonymous, digitalized card, into the hand of the guest checking in. The room number can be written on the inside of what is essentially a folded napkin for your key or card. Discreet and, in my opinion, mandatory.

And all thanks to women.

Still, I can't help wonder why the hotels of the world don't humanize the check-in process. Both genders will love you for it. As someone who's on the road so often, there are few things that bug me more than standing in line waiting to check into my pre-paid room. Wouldn't it make sense for the employee behind the counter to come out from behind the desk, take your credit card, and check you in using a small portable apparatus, the way they do across European restaurants and coffee shops? It's secure, discreet, speedy, and the customer doesn't have to worry, as she might in a restaurant, that some errant employee has kidnapped her Visa or American Express card and is busy making multiple imprints for himself and all his buddies.

Shall we head upstairs?

I have a friend named Pam Dillon who travels a lot, both for business and pleasure. As an extraordinarily successful female executive—she held starring roles at Goldman Sachs and J.P. Morgan before starting her own business—Pam has been collecting experiences at luxury hotels throughout the world for years. At one point in her life, Pam spent two weeks out of every month on the road. She didn't stick to one particular hotel, but preferred to sample as many different hotels as possible. These days, Pam is on the road for about a month or two a year. As a female who collects hotels the way some guys collect golf courses, I want her input here.

"So Pam," I say, "how do you feel about a bellhop—usually a guy—taking control of your luggage? We're talking about your most private and essential stuff here."

For most men, bellhops are a nonissue. The choice is simple: Let the guy lug your stuff, or do it yourself. For females, the issue is more complicated.

"I don't like it," Pam says immediately. "Unless I ascertain my luggage isn't at risk"—she beams—"at which point, I love it."

Still, she confesses she would feel more comfortable if the bellhop were female. She doesn't want a man with her in her bedroom—a perfect stranger—telling her how the TV works, even with the door wide open. It feels to her as if a strange guy has invaded a girls' locker room. "It's not a sex thing," Pam says. "It's something more primitive than that—it's a *safety* thing. The same goes for room service," she adds.

I agree: The female bellperson and room service attendant is an idea that's waiting to happen. It's not just some whimsical, gender-bender notion, but a concept that will make countless female hotel visitors feel more at ease. Thanks to the feminine influence across our culture, I know that I'm increasingly conscious of cleanliness, especially when I travel. For all I know, a bellman's hand could be one of the filthiest places inside a hotel. You can't exactly ask, "Do you squirt hand sanitizer on your fingers in between jobs?" or whip out a pair of hospital gloves. But in an era of swine flu and SARS, I'd rather not have a male stranger handling my baggage, either.

Also, in their quest for tips, many male bellmen are aggressive, even pushy, in their desire to take over a guest's luggage. It can feel like being held up at gunpoint. A female traveler can easily feel bullied into handing over her most private belongings. As we'll see throughout these pages, females trust other females more. Thus, a female bellperson staff would go a long way toward assuaging any anxiety a woman might have about surrendering her luggage and clothing.

On the topic of luggage, you can credit the female of the species with the invention of the rolling suitcase. The number of female passengers who travel with rolling suitcases and pull fifty manageable pounds with them is on the increase. Meaning that a female, if she wants, can bring multiple pairs of shoes with her, and transport the weight herself, like a small caboose. For women, and for anyone over a certain age, wheels make life, and cumbrous transport, possible—and in many cases, eliminate the need to hand your bags over to a young man you've never met, no matter how swell he looks in his bellboy outfit.

I slip the plastic digitalized key in the lock, a sudden green illumination flickers, and we're in.

First things first: I can't help but notice the gorgeous bed, one that's fit for a deposed princess or, at the very least, a foot-weary female who thinks of herself as one. In 1999, the Westin Hotel chain rolled out, and trademarked, the Heavenly Bed. Angel wing white, covered with a plump duvet, its sheets boast a staggering thread count (whatever that is). The pillows are first-rate, too, and there are many more of them than a single traveler or even a lazing family needs.

Many hotels seem to have finally recognized the importance of pillows—and that if you meet a female traveler's pillow needs, there's a good chance she'll remain faithful to you for life. For people who travel regularly, a good pillow can make the difference between a good and a mediocre night's sleep. All things being equal, if you're looking for leverage, or customer loyalty, knowing that a guest always gets the correct pillows (soft, hard, or medium) may be an important dimension of whether or not she elects to come back to your hotel.

When the actress Elizabeth Taylor travels, she rents out the entire floor, as do many oil-rich Middle Eastern dignitaries. Yes, it's expensive, but as an antipaparazzi measure, few things can compare. Plus, there's always the issue of hygiene, which is why Madame Chiang Kai-shek, the wife of the Chairman of the Nationalist Government of China, brought her own linens with her when she and her husband stayed at Blair House while visiting the Roosevelts—a gesture that apparently riled Eleanor Roosevelt to no end.

Let's look around. The first thing Pam notices in a hotel room is whether or not the FF&E—industry speak for furniture, fixtures, and equipment—is more than two to three years old. A good hotel replaces soft things like sheets and pillowcases a lot faster than a bad hotel does. Just as, if not more, important than updated FF&E?

Cleanliness.

"The room doesn't have to be fancy," Pam tells me. "But it has to have a feeling about it of *clean*. It must smell good and it must be clean. Intellectually I know full well that someone has been in that room before me—but I don't want to feel it. I don't want to smell them. I don't want someone else's *trace* to be there."

I'm not surprised!

Aside from cleanliness, another important issue for women, as I pointed out earlier, has to do with air quality and their ability to adjust the temperature in a hotel room. Whether or not it's physiological—since females are generally more susceptible to variations in cold and hot than men are, or whether women unconsciously resent some hotel-chain chieftain, presumably male, determining the baseline temperature for her room—it's something women notice. Without control, a woman feels teed off, suffocated, and yes, oppressed. Even if management gets it right, and the female guest plans on keeping the temperature as it is, she appreciates—no, make that *really strongly insists upon*—having the option to raise up or lower the temp a notch.

"And whatever I want to regulate in my hotel room, I want it to be *easy,*" Pam says. "I don't want to take a technology course. I just want the thing to work. Don't give me a gadget, give me control! That's what a remote control is—control! Also, I don't like feeling claustrophobic. What a hotel of the future will do is bring the outside in, so that the natural world and the indoor world mix and merge, while still making me feel safe."

Inside the room, there's a cutting-edge, easy-to-use, flat-screen TV. It declutters the dresser, giving the room an airier, more spacious feeling than it had in the days of those old twenty-nine-inch color Zeniths with the attached VCR-DVD player. Instead of a brown BarcaLounger, a fainting couch perches across from the bed. As for the walls, the artwork is jazzier and more decorative than the usual windmills, silos, and generic coast of Maine shorelines you once found in most hotels. These days you're more likely to find a Matisse, Miró, or Magritte poster adorning the walls, reflecting the sophistication and education level of the guests the hotel hopes to attract. Even the minibar seems to be tailor-made less for the scotch-and-soda guy than for the knowledgeable female who, don't get me wrong, savors the small indulgences of life, including chocolate, but prefers them in lighter, healthier portions.

When Pam was headquartered for a time in upstate New York and spending a lot of time in Manhattan, she tried out and rejected a lot of cutting-edge hotels. Places that were designed, often dazzlingly, by men, but that failed to take into account the needs of female travelers and, in some cases, of human beings in general. One of these experiences took place at the W Hotel, off Union Square. "They concentrate on style—not people," Pam says.

"What do you mean by that?" I ask.

"Well, I really love a lot of things they do at the W, but I must say, every edge is hard. Every color is cool. There are no earth tones. They *think* they have earth tones, but when an earth tone has that much gray in it, it's not an earth tone anymore. There's nothing even *faux*-personal in any of the rooms. You don't walk into one of these hotels and say, *Wow, I feel comfortable*. You walk in and say, *Wow, I feel cool*. It makes you feel like swinging open the minibar and pouring yourself a vodka."

Stunning though it may be, the newly renovated Gramercy Park Hotel was only a slight improvement, Pam said. "I felt kind of groovy the first night. But the next day, getting ready for my meeting, I felt a lot less so, since the lighting in the bathroom was so poor I had a hard time getting ready. Plus, all the furniture is designed for someone who stands about a foot taller than I am. The owners want a hotel room to *look* a certain way—they don't seem to care as much how a person feels when she's *in* it."

Cutting-edge design, checkerboard floors, and a chance sighting of Brad and Angelina in the lobby aren't what Pam, or, in my experience, most women, are seeking when they check into a hotel. They're looking for safety, cleanliness, serenity, and comfort. In fact, they're after what their own homes should feel like and often don't. "What exactly do you mean by 'comfort,' Pam?" I ask.

"Earth tones," Pam replies firmly. "It also has to do with the way some things are shaped."

In her hotel bedroom, Pam wants round. She wants curvy. She wants soft.

Our next stop is the bathroom.

For many women, the hotel bathroom can either make or break a stay. The hotel bathroom is the one room that you want to be at least as good—make that better—than the one you have at home. On the top of Pam's list for a superior hotel bathroom? Good, efficient, warm lighting. "I don't know why first-class hotels don't have switches for both indoor and outdoor light," Pam says, "because that's something women would go *crazy* for."

"Why?" I ask.

"Because most women have figured out through trial and error how to put their cosmetics on in their home bathrooms, no matter how dark or light it is outside. It's an issue women face, literally, every single day. Men don't realize that women have to think about cosmetics and hair and whether or not they can see themselves properly, and how it will look outside. Dimmers would make me a lot more comfortable if I weren't so afraid my makeup would look stupid outside in the natural light."

Of all the stats we've examined in our work with hotels, this much stands out to me: What's most important for the female traveler is what amenities a hotel offers. Does a free bathing cap and a minibottle of A-plus conditioner matter terribly much to me or to most men I know? I can't say I even notice them. But amenities like these make a difference to women, and hotels are making definite progress in this regard. Pam even cares about the *quality* of the hotel soap—and gets ticked off when it leaves residue on her skin, because it has not been matched up with how hard or soft the local water is. Now and again, she admits, she'll also take something home with her, e.g., a shampoo that her hair reacts well to.

Aside from the hair dryer, let's pause for a second to appreciate a decidedly female-friendly new touch: the bowed shower curtain. Rather than attaching straight across the perimeter of the bath, the curtain gently luffs out, giving the bather an additional eight inches of space and oxygen. The result: The shower feels less clammy, and claustrophobic, and the female guest need never make physical contact with the actual curtain. With an old-fashioned, straight-across shower curtain, there's always the perception it's been touched, or contaminated somehow, by countless other guests. By never touching you, the bowed shower curtain deftly sidesteps the gross-out factor. No big deal? For women, it is a big deal. No female I know wants that curtain getting anywhere *near* her.

"Do environmental niceties in a hotel matter to you, Pam?" I ask. "Do you appreciate those virtuous LCD lightbulbs?"

"I like hotels that are energy-conscious. I like the idea that someone is being thoughtful."

"How do you feel about those notes hotels put on your pillow that tell you that you can choose between not getting your sheets and pillowcases washed for environmental purposes, or you can get them laundered every night?"

"Oh, that is often such *crap*. So many of the hotels that leave those notes are the same ones who waste energy in so many ways."

"So what would the female-friendly hotel room of the future be/look like/act like—say, the Pam Dillon DNA Plaza Pavilion of 2050?"

Pam thinks for a moment. "The room would be customized to *me*. However they are going to get that info, it's going to give me less of an impression that a gazillion people have stayed in that room before me. Somehow—now don't ask me how—there would be *Pam* stuff in there when I arrive—customized pillows, soft linen, soft towels. I want the hotelier to know my preferences, but at the same time I don't want to feel as though I've been invaded. So my dream hotel should figure out a way to do that."

I know what Paco stuff is. It would be a Scandinavian-style bed where the top covers are not tucked in, the better to accommodate a tall guy who doesn't like getting his feet scrunched up at the bottom. There would be a few books, crime thrillers and biographies mostly. There would be a bottle of my favorite single-malt scotch. Oh, and Dreamboat would be there, too.

Recently, I read that the Hampton Inn in Albany, New York, rolled out the concept of "A Floor of Her Own"—a floor devoted exclusively to female guests, with (shades of boarding school) male guests permitted on the floor only on weekends. The idea is to make female travelers feel private and secure, and give them the opportunity to network in peace and without distraction. Amenities offered include skin moisturizers, hand creams, and fuzzy socks; and a hospitality suite filled with cookies, exotic coffees, high-end teas, and magazines, accessible only via a special electronic key. It's an unusual concept. It feels a little like affirmative action with a terrycloth bathrobe thrown in. I could imagine as many women going for it as not.

The Nob Hill Lambourne, a boutique San Francisco hotel, has gotten into the act by enticing the female traveler with a complimentary "rebalancing basket" (it includes workout barbells, bottled water, exercise mats, and yoga videos), as well as a full line of for-sale homeopathic remedies. If you're missing your children, the Lambourne gives its regular guests a free daily fifteen-minute domestic phone call to the kids, as well as a framed photo of the little ones every time Mom checks into the hotel, plus a free San Francisco toy she can tuck inside her suitcase before departure. New at the mothering business, and feeling uncertain? If you stay at the "Mommy Nest" suite at the Parrot Mill Inn in Chatham, New Jersey, the price of admission includes a small army of lactation consultants. There are also "procreation vacation" packages for couples who need a break, as well as "babymoons" for couples in the final weeks of a pregnancy (the expectant father gets champagne; the mother makes do with cider).

But how would someone like Pam Dillon, who's worked around men for most of her professional career, feel about staying in a females-only hotel? "I would certainly be open-minded. If it's delivered right, it could be very calming. In my imagination, it would have a public space of some kind. Natural light. Good lighting. Very relaxed. Again, no male hard edges. Women just want to feel relaxed. I don't want to feel on the cutting edge of technology. Don't get me wrong—I love lots of modern things, and I like being on the cutting edge intellectually. Just not in my *hotel room*."

Finally, Pam, do you care to comment on the hotel restaurant, where the menu typically accommodates the alpha-male traveler—lots of organ meats in portions that could feed an elephant and her calf?

In my own travels, I've found a way around this by cherry-picking stuff on the menu. I'll take the basmati rice that comes with the steak and the asparagus that goes with the porterhouse, and the Kobe beef hamburger with a side of broccoli, rather than the French fries. It's not all that inconvenient for the kitchen. They can't really refuse, either, since the food is already cooked, and on hand.

Pam has found her own way around this dilemma. "I order two appetizers."

So do a lot of women, I've noticed in my travels. Many, many heart attacks later, the days of the scotch-and-soda man and the giant four-egg breakfast special with hash browns is over. So why haven't many hotels adapted to the nutritional, health-oriented needs of both the female and the male of the species? Everything on the hotel menu doesn't have to be drenched in cheese and butter or corn syrup; fast-food restaurants already fill that role nicely. Smaller portions, vegetables, fruits, juices other than orange—is there anybody out there?

I hope you have a nice stay.

8

THE FEMALE, UNPLUGGED

I'm standing in a strip mall—it could be just about anywhere.

Two hundred yards away, the Best Buy is hard to miss. There is a Target on one side, and a panini chain with outdoor seating to the other, but this colossus, with its brick siding, glass panes, big angular fin of navy blue, and signature yellow price tag, stands out as prominently as a college hockey rink. From a design perspective, it's about as architecturally male a structure as exists—all flatness and hard, uncomely angles. There's nothing about the exterior that announces to an uninitiated visitor what could possibly reside inside the place. Futons? Speedboats? Used cars? It could even be a private men's club, with the emphasis on "men's."

A small but poignant illustration of male-female confusion is taking place right before my eyes. A man and a woman are approaching the Best Buy at exactly the same time. Once inside the threshold, or decompression zone (that slightly dimmed region a consumer enters before reaching the second set of portals), our guy veers without hesitation to the right. He's come here before, no doubt about that, and knows where to go, whereas the female drifts to the left, not realizing she's about to run smack up against the glass door marked "exit."

Whoops. Wrong way. Now she turns to follow the man through the *right* door and onto the floor.

Appearances—in this case, the almost comically male exterior of this and other Best Buys across the country—are deceptive. Like a lot of other big box stores, Best Buy is making a valiant effort to make the female of the species feel more comfortable once she's inside. In fact, there's even an individual at Best Buy's home office who heads up the store's "Feminization Team."

Let's go in.

"Welcome to Best Buy," says the young bearded fellow in the kiosk by the door. He's in charge of store "shrink," better known as theft. Among his responsibilities is to make sure that the receipt the cashier handed you, and the giant item inside your shopping cart, matches up as you leave the store.

"Thanks," I say.

The female influence starts . . . *now.*

A survey published not long ago by the Consumer Electronics Association estimates that nearly half of all electronic purchases in the United States are made by females. That makes sense to me, though I suspect the figure runs even higher. At the same time, many retailers are aware that women consumers shy away from big box electronics stores because a) there's too much stuff to choose from; and b) there's not enough personalized service, even if she manages to hunt down an employee knowledgeable enough to help her. So instead of physically shopping a Best Buy, many females go online instead, research the TV or the laptop in question, do some back-and-forth comparison shopping, then either order the product online or march into the store armed with some solid facts and figures.

Historically, food and so-called soft goods, such as bed sheets and apparel, have been marketed to women, whereas hard goods—TVs, computers, cars, even blenders—have been marketed to men. A longstanding issue we face at Envirosell, whether we're working for Samsung or for Nokia, is, *How do stores make these same hard goods relevant to females—when for women, the* "cool" *factor doesn't much matter?*

Over the course of our work within the consumer electronic industries, again and again we've found there to be a direct correlation between the success of a store and the number of female employees working on the floor. It was a lesson that first came to our attention when we worked for Radio Shack in the 1990s. This issue is particularly noticeable within a mall setting. Since most mall concourses are crowded with women, wouldn't it make sense, we asked Radio Shack, to dramatically increase the number of female employees? They did, and it worked very well for them. Male consumers are charmed, as well. Men are much less threatened by a female techie than a female might potentially be cowed by a male techie.

But why—just asking—would your average female prefer interacting with a member of her own gender?

The short answer? Women trust women more. They feel chances are less likely a female employee will sell them something just for the sake of a higher sales commission. Plus, women don't like to pick up even the merest whiff that a male employee is in any way talking down his nose to them. A female consumer's level of confidence and savvy plays a critical part in how she approaches asking for help or advice. For a novice female electronics buyer, interacting with a female employee who may recognize and understand her own uncertainty beats talking to a young man who might get snappy with her (not that a lot of male consumers aren't as technologically challenged as many females).

A few years ago, Best Buy went so far as to open a prototype store directly targeted for females in a suburb of Chicago. Among its focuses was in-store education. The store had actual classroom space, a worktable, and chairs. The notion behind it was both simple and strategic: The more females are taught how to use technology, the more technology they will consider and maybe even consume. If Best Buy could teach a woman how to use a digital camera and link it to a specialized printer, she would realize how easy it is to, say, create and crop her own photos or customize her own line of greeting cards. In the long run, she might even trade up. Apple stores do the same thing with iLife and iWeb classes. I even know of a Whole Foods that holds its own yoga classes. In general, the more a female customer can see beyond the technological specs of a digital camera—the 8.0 megapixel CCD, the 4X optical, image-stabilized zoom, and so on—the more she can envisage a fantasy scenario, even a lifestyle.

Bear in mind, too, that the actual information on packaging is a terrific way to justify, as well as distract from, price.

If you ask Best Buy management, their female-targeted prototype store was a big success. I'm not sure why it closed down. But Best Buy's impulses were, and are, sound and smart.

Having cleared security, the presence of females within the store is seemingly, and subtly, everywhere.

For starters, the voice on the overhead speakers telling customers about the Geek Squad is female.

The very first individual to greet me is a smiling young female store manager, who asks if she can help direct us anywhere. No thanks, we're just looking.

Glance up—oh! and while you're at it, glance *deep* into the store, too. Every piece of visual signage in this Best Buy—the twenty-foot-long photo on the far wall of the young woman lounging on a bed in noise-reduction headphones; the college-age couple snuggling on a couch, watching a movie on a big-screen TV together; even the photograph adorning the selection of wall speakers, in which a female sits by a young man as he cheers on his favorite baseball team—is part of Best Buy's attempt to transform hardware from a tech-minded boys' club into a female-friendly (or at least gender-neutral) retail experience. From the store manager to the females beaming down from the walls, these touches are designed to inject a hint of sensuality and intimacy to an environment known for product specs, row after row of TVs, and pods of teenagers killing time by trying out the latest incarnation of "Rock Band."

Some fifteen feet into the store, the first product display we run into is a tableful of digital cameras. There must be forty or fifty, in all shapes, colors, sizes, and price points. Note that the table on which they sit is not rectangular. It has no hard edges; instead, it gently waves and undulates. That said, it would be simplistic to posit that male design is exclusively comprised of angles and hard surfaces, whereas females are helplessly enticed by soft corners and curves or at least by a pleasing ambiguity of design. But in this statement is the kernel—the smallest beginning—of a truth that continues to evolve within the retail design world.

Around Envirosell, we have a saying that's become almost a Zen koan: Women buy technology and consumer electronics not as supersonic 007-gadgets, as men do, but as tools and applications that facilitate relationships and enhance their lives. Over and over again, I tell my technology clients that men buy instruments of technology, whereas women buy instruments of relationship. Women relate to computers as interactive and collaborative. They form a relationship with them and with the websites that they browse. Guys, on the other hand, tend to go for all the bells and whistles—the 2.4 GHz Intel Core Duo processor with 3MB on-chip shared L2 cache, the diagonal antiglare widescreen TFT LED backlit display, the 250GB 5400-rpm Serial ATA hard drive (I don't know what any of these things mean, but they sure sound like they might help you get the job done faster).

Among the reasons that Circuit City and Comp USA floundered is that they were selling technology as opposed to electronics or appliances. Circuit City, for one, exploded in the 1990s. Employees were compensated by commission. Each employee team was assigned a certain section within the store. In effect, everyone who worked there was competing against everyone else who worked there. As such, a Circuit City employee had very little incentive to suggest to the consumer that once she'd sprung for an expensive TV, why didn't she take a look at the matching TV stands a couple of sections away?

In my opinion, Circuit City and CompUSA crashed because they simply didn't recognize the changing face of the consumer. Both were too male and too geeky. They ran their businesses like consumer electronics versions of auto parts stores. The midwestern-based Best Buy was much faster to pick up on the new consumer—the female—and what she wanted: education, interaction, and the sense that she wasn't on the verge of getting hustled wherever she turned.

It's no coincidence that one of the very first things Best Buy employees tell a consumer is that they're not working on a commission basis, and that if they're called away, any other employee in the store can help them. It takes the heat off the customer, who knows she's not being pressured or played. Again, this low-sell approach was the result of Best Buy's attempt to differentiate the company from Circuit City. Instead of employees working on commission, management sets standards or benchmarks for various sections of a store. To this day, employee bonuses are based on the success of the team rather than the individual.

Still, in terms of the female consumer, I'm puzzled by how few ready-built tableaux there are in this Best Buy. Time and again, we've found that a good way to sell to women is by engaging their imaginations. As with the digital cameras, women enjoy visualizing what role a product will play in their lives, and how it will enable them and their families to enjoy a certain kind of lifestyle. Some women consumers enjoy imagining a family gathering, a playroom with comfortable seating so that the whole family can enjoy a good movie. Remember that the male of the species is spending his money, while the female is spending her *family's* money.

For example, there's a display of Linksys wireless routers on an end cap in the far reaches of this store. One after another. The specs are writ big. This modem has muscle! But the store has made no attempt to suggest how a female consumer might integrate this Linksys modem into her life. How might it improve it, enhance it, enrich it? Might it just maybe provide a faster e-mail connection to her loved ones who live far away?

In general, men want to know: *What is this technology? Is it cool? Is it powerful?*

In general, women want to know: *What and where does this get me/us?*

This same issue extends to the TV section. Inside many Best Buys is a Magnolia home theater. It's set up as though you've already transported the thing home and installed it in your living room, finished basement, or upstairs nook. The screen sits flush against the wall. Two comfy armchairs sit across from it. There's a coffee table, too, where the remote control sits. It's a neat attempt to overcome the TV section, where the Sonys, Panasonics, Denons, and Samsungs are lined up, one after another, like shiny rectangular crows on a wire. In that environment, they're pretty much indistinguishable.

Let's head over to the computer section.

When a female buys a laptop, very often she will choose a model based on how much it weighs. Unfortunately, with laptops, there is rarely any correlation between size and weight. As I wander through the laptop aisle, I'm struck more by what I'm *not* seeing. It's a shame, for example, that there's no big sign here that says, *This is our lightest model!* A stat like that would score big points with female consumers.

One aisle over, Best Buy showcases a rack of computer bags, a stylin' alternative to your basic black satchel. These bags are colorful, striped, and distinctive. But the nearby mirror hanging from a hook is too small and narrow for a female to see how her new bag might look hanging off her shoulder. A missed opportunity—too bad.

Earlier, I mentioned what a good idea in-store education is. Even out-of-store education is an ingenious selling point, as well as an addition to the bottom line. Back in 2003, Best Buy bought a small midwestern company known as the Geek Squad, a collection of signature blue-shirted young men and women whose job it is to eliminate the anxiety consumers associate with purchasing a big-ticket item. If you sign up for one of their service plans (and they don't come cheap), Geek Squad members will do everything but reshingle your house. They'll set up your computer router. They'll wrap and conceal your wires. They'll install your home theater, make sure the woofer and the tweeter are working right, and that the orange-tipped DVD cord goes where it's supposed to go. If you want to hang your huge new TV on the wall across from your bed using bracket arms, that's no problem, either. The service even extends to GPS devices and satellite radios.

Naturally, among the Geek Squad's other jobs is to convince consumers that now that they've spent all this money for a new home theater, don't they want first-rate speakers to go with it, as well as the highest-end cables and cords? All those extras maximize your home theater-watching experience and Best Buy's service offerings are the company's fastest-growing segment.

Take note of another discreet touch designed to appeal to the female.

A young couple is paying for their purchase, perhaps a fancy new plasma set for their first house or apartment. They're huddled together on a bench, with the Best Buy employee catty-corner to them. A computer screen listing the item and all the gear that goes with it, plus the applicable sales tax, faces all three of them. It's an example of total transparency. I can't help but think of the model rolled out by Sephora, the cosmetics and skincare chain, which transformed the customer experience by having the employee and the customer on the same side of the counter. Though the actual closing is done at a classic cash register, with the in-store interaction you and the Sephora employee are on the same team. It's a model that encourages intimacy and collaboration. There's no *Me* versus *Them* factor. The experience thus becomes close-knit and transactional—a plus for the female consumer.

Even though we haven't bought anything, let's head for the exit.

Best Buy has managed its checkout wonderfully well. In fact, it's the most profitable area of the store. How and why? By funneling customers into one line, as opposed to three or four separate queues, consumers are shepherded along a single corridor lined left and right with impulse items designed to appeal to both genders. There's everything here from Warcraft cards and AAA batteries to snacks and cold drinks to beauty products like Burt's Bees lip gloss and colorful gift bags that light up like a family of fireflies when you press a button.

What would be even better here is a big, can't-miss-it sign announcing to the female customer (and the male customer, too) that some big, strapping Best Buy employee with a metal dolly will load your heavy purchase into your car. I've watched women in the aisles of Best Buy struggling with weight. Men don't realize the extent to which the idea of lugging something can sometimes make all the difference between a product a woman buys and a product she can't imagine hoisting into the backseat of her car, much less how the heck she's going to get the thing into her house. An enormous sign offering free transport to your car would literally and figuratively take a huge burden off of anyone's shoulders, female *and* male.

I want to make one final stop before we leave: the women's bathroom. I grab our smiley female store manager and ask if she can confirm that the coast is clear.

This Best Buy ladies' room is better than most—clean, airy, and marbled. Best Buy has made an attempt to break up any institutional hard edges by perching a large, leafy plant between the two sinks, an attempt to inject some animation and personality into all that cold-hearted marble. Other Best Buy restrooms, the manager tells me, are superior, and even feature decorative lighting—this one just isn't there yet.

Mark my words: It will be.

Question: How do most *men* react to the increasing female influence in a fabled Boys Town like Best Buy? They probably don't even notice it. And in some respects, the question is moot, since Best Buy already has a winning franchise with males. The Geek Squad is a terrific concept for the tech-challenged man. It makes him feel better about his own handyman inadequacies—*Only Geeks would know how to do this stuff.* Adapting it to the tech-challenged female presents a different problem. One key solution would be to assign more female geeks to the mix. A female digerati interpreter (or a whole bunch of them) is a canny idea whose time has come.

I can't get that rounded digital camera table out of my mind—the one that greeted me when I entered this Best Buy.

Having interacted with the design professions over the years, I know that design and architecture are two of the last professions to have become gender-integrated. It's hard to name a female architect before 1970. If we do find one, it's because she was married to someone else. My friend Elle Chute, who runs a strategic design and branding company out of Columbus, Ohio, is part of the leading edge in a transformation that's taking place in the retail design industry—borne of her long-held belief that physical environments impact people both physically and emotionally.

Place a person in a long line at an airport, Elle tells me, and she'll feel like throttling the person behind the desk. Put that same person inside a cathedral and the thought would never occur to her.

Elle and her company once worked for a U.S. convenience store chain called Sheetz that also features great made-to-order foods and coffee. Elle's goal was to make women feel more comfortable in a convenience store, while at the same time retaining the male customer.

"For the men, we gave the stores more of a renovated factory look—raw materials and galvanized metals," Elle recalls. "At the same time, for the female, we got rid of the harsh seats and provided more circular, curved places to sit. We created booths that were rounded. We softened both the colors and the overhead lighting. Then we counterbalanced that with more angular, raw-type finishes. In interviews we did with females after that, women really did feel really great in that space."

That said, Elle agrees that it isn't as simplistic as *Men Equal Hard Angles* versus *Women Equal Curves.* In many cases, she says, women simply prefer store design that's less monochromatic, more varied, more pattern-filled.

"On a recent trip to Argentina," Elle goes on, "I was struck as I walked through the street markets by how differently men and women shopped. It dawned on me that the same is true in stores, too. Both parties may approach the store with a goal, and the male will generally continue on his path. But watch a woman, and while she may start with a single purpose, the environment stimulates her in a different way: sights, sounds, and colors activate her senses. She slows her stride, enlarges her pathways. Her brain is cued to remember other tasks she can accomplish during this trip. While she spends more time, and may appear to be more leisurely, she actually is using her time wisely, and when she thinks back on this day, she'll feel smart and productive. I think this is why shopping is in many ways more satisfying and relaxing for women than for men.

"That may be why female designers tend to think of space more holistically," Elle goes on. "Often I have had to say, 'No, a store isn't about angles, it's an integrated whole' to male designers, who seem to think, 'If I can just make this store bigger, it'll be more successful.' The thing is, it often doesn't work that way."

Everywhere you look these days, from fashion boutiques to the pharmacy sections of drugstores, you can find evidence of deliberately female-friendly store design. It's curved. It's circular. It's soft-edged. It's environmentally mindful. It emphasizes wood, rather than stainless steel. Nor are the rooms in the store or showroom necessarily square boxes. The light is flattering and the chairs are hospitable. Even the fixtures on the walls have rounded edges. It's as though someone woke up one day, and said, *Wait, hold on, you mean the world doesn't have to be made up of straight lines and hard angles?* I attribute this softening to the feminization of design.

Envirosell isn't in the business of store design. Sure, we can go to Exxon Mobil and say that we've observed women having trouble with their gas pumps and the interfaces on the machine, and they'll take our advice. We can go to H&M and ask, "Who designed that gloomy dressing room? Would you really want your wife or girlfriend or daughter trying on clothes in there?" and they'll look into it. Interestingly, the convenience store, or C-store, uses the same marketing term used to describe females' tastes in wine and liquor: *Light, bright, and white.* If you look at the new Exxon Mobil and BP convenience stores, the emphasis on cleanliness is pronounced—and I have to think my first book, *Why We Buy,* had a little something to do with that (I'm happy to say the C-store community took that book to heart). Both Exxon Mobil and BP have worked hard to make their new stations female-friendly. The pumps and islands are well covered and brightly lit and, along with the attached convenience stores, have been designed for easy cleaning. For in-company-owned stations, keeping the premises clean is a big priority. In our interviews with women, the new stations have been a big hit in the United States, Germany, the United Kingdom, and Ireland. (Then again, I remember Arco's CEO telling me that the company eliminated paper towels at the gas pump as a cost-saving exercise, in spite of our documenting the large number of women who used them to get the smell of gas off their hands or to wipe off the grease after pumping.)

Another bonus, or irony, depending on how you look at it, is that when the average C-store cleans, lightens, and brightens up its act, while it gains huge points with the female customer it loses big-time with teenage boys, who no longer view the place as a rockin' hang-out spot.

Where does all this leave, say, a large home repair or office chain, or any other store where, trapped within twelve-foot-high shelves, it's all too easy for a female to get creeped out? And women *do* get creeped out in places that are too big, where they feel alone, and they can't see the door and any other customers nearby. Will these places someday go the way of the specialty store? It's very possible. I can imagine it now: a circular room. Squishy chairs. A curving display of mobile phone holders. Not thirty printers, but maybe five. Not twenty-five cameras, but maybe three. And a beautifully rounded, ribbon-shaped display of Epson and Hewlett-Packard products.

Try that, and a woman won't think twice when she forks over twenty-five bucks for a single black ink-jet cartridge.

9

WOMEN AND SIN

Remember the Seven Deadly Sins? A quick Google search serves up a timely reminder: lust, gluttony, greed, sloth, wrath, envy, and pride.

The notion of women and vice doesn't include any sins on the above list (and by vice, understand that I'm not talking about a scenario where a uniformed officer ends up dragging a female off in leg chains, either). Instead, I'm talking about the ways in which women have influenced and even transformed certain everyday pleasures, ones that enhance many of our lives. This time around, rather than concentrating on her multitasking self, I want to focus instead on those moments and hours when the contemporary female drops all those balls she has up in the air and devotes herself to escape.

We'll be making four stops this morning. We'll drop by a casino, mull over the question of females and food, pay a visit to our local liquor store, then finally stop by the drugstore chain to stare at the wall of cigarettes on display behind the cash/wrap.

Onward.

SIN #1: LUCK BE A LADY

Welcome to Las Vegas. While Nevada may lead the country in its sheer number of casinos—the state has some 370 sin palaces—remember that out of America's fifty states, all but eight of them currently have casinos, both offshore and on. Even staid old Massachusetts has been flirting with the idea. And casinos don't comprise the whole gaming landscape, which also includes horse tracks, dog tracks, resorts, and cruise ships.

As a human fascination, gaming is extremely old. Dice have been excavated from Egyptian tombs. As early as 2300 B.C., all cultures, from the Chinese to the Romans, were known to play games involving dexterity and chance. Let's not forget that in the early 1700s, the British colonization of America itself was partially funded by winnings from lotteries, or "voluntary taxation," as gambling was known back then.

The American casino business is an industry that was originally set up, owned, and operated by men—not a surprise when you think about it. Yet a healthy chunk of the industry today is made up of female gamblers. A magic moment in the gaming industry came when the casinos realized they were making more income off slot machines than they were off table and card games. To put it more bluntly, they were making more money off of the female player than they were off the male ones.

Until the late 1980s, slot machines served the same purpose as a well-positioned bench or chair serves for men in the context of a department or specialty store—except this time around, the slot machines were places in which to keep female gamblers occupied while the men were out on the tables losing money on blackjack, craps, keno, baccarat, or what have you. A tumbler of rye whiskey, a little nerve, a medium-size bet—and the guy goes home poorer and probably no wiser.

Again, into the 1980s, the casino industry thought about retail only in terms of a place for the male winners, or more likely losers, where they could buy "forgive me" gifts for their mates. The ascendancy of slots, and the importance of good retail, has fundamentally transformed the American casino business. The Forum Shops at Caesars is one of the most successful shopping malls in the world. The shopping venues at the Venetian and, most recently, Wynn, are breathtaking examples of the importance of the female visitor. In a stunning reversal of roles, today the gaming tables have become parking lots for the men, while the women plug the dollars and coins (and these days, prepaid cards) into slot machines.

Certainly casinos were well aware that as of 1992, gross gambling revenue in the United States, which represents the amount wagered minus the amount paid to players, before taxes, and includes income from the commercial casino industry as well as from lotteries, legal bookmaking, bingo, Indian reservations, and card games, was $58.2 billion. And that in 2007, the last time gross gambling revenue was measured, it was $92.3 billion. The top five casino markets across the United States are the Las Vegas Strip, followed in order by Atlantic City, Chicagoland (which spreads across both Indiana and Illinois), Connecticut, and Detroit.

Among the female-friendly lures of this successful and surprising evolution has been the deliberate theming of slot machines to evoke women's nostalgic memories for the television shows they probably watched growing up—1960s TV fare such as *Gilligan's Island, The Beverly Hillbillies,* and *I Dream of Jeannie,* as well as popular long-running daytime game shows like *Wheel of Fortune, Jeopardy!,* and *The Price Is Right.*

A few years ago I went on a fascinating retreat weekend with the creative team at IGT, a company based in Reno that designs and manufactures slot machines. We were mulling over ideas for possible future gaming machines. Our goal was to come up with concepts that both facilitated team play and permitted individual play.

As the female has become the biggest moneymaker for the casino industry, the slot machine has become less about gambling and more about entertainment. The one-armed bandit of the 1950s has turned into a pleasure machine for the twenty-first century. All the nuances of the experience have been deconstructed. While the machine is designed to pay out a certain percentage of the money that's been plugged in, and the fancier the casino the lower that number is, the machine is also designed to give the player the experience of getting close to the jackpot. Another major innovation has been multiple-play features that let you make more than one bet at a time. The big moneymaker for the casino has been the penny machines. No, you don't play a penny at a time, but you have the basic building block of a penny within a multiple bet game. Thus, like playing multiple bingo cards, the machine demands a certain concentration that makes it easier to get lost in. The penny machines are particularly popular with women.

Adding to this evolution has been the recognition on the part of casinos that if females are making such good money for casinos, then shouldn't they make their star gender feel more at home? Today the seats you can find in a contemporary casino are plush and comfortable. There are no straight-backed office chairs or ratty red bar stools. There are even places for females to hang their purses. Instead of coins, prestocked cards have come into the equation, a concession both to labor cost and to sanitation. (Hear that word "clean" again?)

From this point, is it any surprise to find the introduction of the loyalty card, which tracks your winnings? When you think about it, the modern casino is an unholy mixture of gambling and loyalty and the loyalty card is another way the casino tracks the individual players and gives them perks based on the amount of money they are wagering. In the same way the male high rollers at the tables have traditionally found themselves comped with free suites, limo rides, and God knows what else, the female who's just gambled away a hundred dollars might find herself gifted with a free five-dollar coupon off the buffet spread that night. Free, that is, if she doesn't think about how much the coupon *really* cost her.

Upstairs, in the hotel portion of the casino, if the female and her significant other are spending the night, when she turns on the TV, she'll find a female explaining the rules and intricacies of every single game, from craps to blackjack. It's not what you might think. The casinos aren't trying to wean the female away from the slot machines. She's too good, natural, and dependable a customer. No, it's more that the average female gambler might feel a tad awkward or uncomfortable at a largely all-male gaming table, even if the dealer is female. Above all, the hotel-casino has a powerfully vested interest in making women feel comfortable within the *overall* casino environment. Like it or not, the traditional role for the female on the gaming floor has been as arm candy. Thus, when she checks into her room, a female tele-educator, as opposed to a cigar-chomping stooge with a voice like Louis Prima's, goes a very long way toward making her feel at home.

Once back in front of the wall of slot machines, the female is content. Slots are less public, and more intimate, than gaming tables. There's no way she can really mess up. And the slots area is attended by other females, who serve also as cage cashiers. It's an extremely secure environment for a woman to park herself. Gambling under the guise of entertainment is like sipping an alcohol so sugary and colorful your taste buds are hardly aware of the alcohol underneath, until you find yourself wobbling home.

SIN #2: APPETITE FOR DESTRUCTION

I'm seated at a lunch table just around the corner from my office with a female of my acquaintance. I'm having a cheeseburger with French fries. She's having a salad, with oil and vinegar on the side.

Eating is a very basic human need, it goes without saying, but I'm certainly not the first person to note that many females have a conflicted relationship with food. For most men I know, eating has never come close to approaching the category of a sin. As I noted in an earlier chapter, an aging male's self-esteem (and the world's judgment) is based less on his trim figure and more on his capacity to provide for his spouse and family. It's not always so for women.

If you consider all the things that women do to abuse themselves in the name of looking good, they are legion. Whether it's diet pills, laxatives, speed, or even the impulse to smoke, keeping up appearances is a major female preoccupation and industry. My memory may be playing tricks, but as a guy who came of age in the late 1960s, I recall few women in my circles who ever smoked pot regularly. My guess is they didn't want to deal with the munchies. Eating is inextricably linked to the female sin of self-criticism, and to the self-help book industry, which today is so large it even merits its own category on the *New York Times* Best Seller List. (It hides discreetly under the category of "Hardcover Advice.") I can remember when a woman who was about to move in with me was first unpacking her book collection. About twenty-five of these things tumbled out. They ranged from the humorous—*150 Dates from Hell*—to the poignant—*Finding Love After Age 40* (all I could think of was that she'd ended up with me. Had the book worked, or steered her off-course?).

In the 2004 film *Mean Girls*, there is a scene in which a group of teenage girls are trading self-recriminations. One says, "I hate my calves." Another says, "God, my hips are so huge." This is followed in short order by, "My hairline's weird," "I hate my pores," and the one that makes me laugh, "My nailbeds suck." Would a guy announce any of these things to a roomful of other males? He might think it, but publicly admit it? Not in my experience. Personally, I can't say I'm in the habit of planting myself in front of the mirror and silently cursing out my chin, my nose, or my nailbeds.

The business of exploiting the female's precarious relationship with herself and with her body and face is a multibillion-dollar industry. Since 1997, there has been a 162 percent increase in the total number of cosmetic procedures in the United States. According to the American Society for Aesthetic Plastic Surgery, out of the roughly 10 million surgical and nonsurgical cosmetic procedures performed in 2008, women patients were responsible for 92 percent of them. For years, liposuction was the leading procedure performed on females. In 2008, it came in second to breast augmentation and Botox—part of the nearly $12 billion Americans spent that year on cosmetic procedures.

As for teeth whitening? Including trips to the dentist and over-the-counter teeth-whitening strips, it's a $300 million industry. According to a study commissioned by the American Academy of Cosmetic Dentistry, teeth-whitening procedures have risen 300 percent over the past several years.

One could easily make a convincing argument that the entire diet food and beverage industry has been influenced by, and directly targets, the female. Reduced-fat Triscuits. Lean beef. Low-fat milk. Diet sodas. "Baked" snacks. Even candy manufacturers make it a point to assert that their breath mints are fat-free. Each day, Americans spend an average of $109 million on dieting and diet-related products. A study released by the University of Minnesota found that by the age of nineteen, one-fifth of all college-age females has used diet pills and that beginning to diet doubles a female's chance of someday becoming a smoker. Neither of these stats was true for young males. One report I read online claims that 80 percent of American women say that they're unhappy with their shape and appearance, and that 1 in 2 American females are on a weight-loss diet at any given time. A further 5 percent of these women and 1 percent of males suffer from anorexia, bulimia, or binge eating.

Where does all this female self-doubt and self-flagellation come from? Certainly the cultural imagery that floats before us every day has had some effect on the contemporary woman, whether it's fashion magazines or movie star magazines, all of which celebrate the skinny, the beautiful, and the well-heeled. Added to which, as I noted earlier in this book, many females, particularly mothers, spend their lives wrestling with some form of guilt. Many women I know feel as though they are not doing enough. It's "I can have it all" versus "I can't have it all" followed by "I *can* have it all, but it's a trade-off and someone has to suffer—my partner, my job, my children." Despite their popularity, lifestyle mavens like Martha Stewart have made a lot of females feel worse, rather than better, about themselves. What is it that makes a female's life successful? Is it finding a mate and having progeny? Is it finding accomplishment at work? It's a puzzle.

According to a piece I read in *Newsweek,* studies show that many men are more likely to diet for health reasons or as a result of a health scare, whereas females, who tend to compare their shapes to their friends', typically diet because of social pressures. Women don't often make it easy for other women. They can be cruel about one another, and it starts early on, too. A female's sense of self-worth often has far less to do with what she achieves than with how she looks and with what accoutrements she totes around.

To their credit, some advertisers have tried to make the female of the species feel more at ease. Dove soap has had a very popular campaign featuring "real women." Again, it is a perhaps-unresolvable clash between what the fashion industry says women should look like versus what they actually do.

Our next two sins can't help but be connected to this same occasionally cloudy self-image.

SIN #3: SMOKE GETS IN HER EYES

As I mentioned earlier, the topic of cigarettes and women is in part linked to weight loss. Advertisers have noted this. The female-targeted cigarette tends to be long, thin, and tubular—a blinding-white magic wand capable of curbing appetite and banishing fat molecules. There is no irony that the female of the species typically smokes the 100-millimeter models. A close female friend of mine who doesn't smoke very often always buys Nat Sherman Fantasias when she does. They are 101 millimeters long, skinny, and come in a series of pastel colors. Some of the major, and most nefarious, innovations in the tobacco industry have had to do with targeting the female smoker who's on the fence about her own shape and curves. I don't know any woman who smokes Camel Wides, or for that matter, any other thick, stumpy cigarette. As a brand, Virginia Slims has less to do with Thomas Jefferson and Monticello than it does with attaining an ideal goal, thinness, along the way distracting the female from a slew of fatal health issues.

Smoking a "lite" cigarette is all about becoming a female so airy and pixie-ish she can almost levitate.

Among the many challenges the tobacco industry faces is that as cigarette taxes have increased, fewer cartons get bought. The number of places where a consumer can buy cigarettes has declined, as well, leaving the convenience store as home base to purchase your coffin nails. The second most popular cigarette-distribution centers are drugstores. This has prompted a lot of debate within that industry. Should a place that's ostensibly focused on keeping consumers healthy even be carrying cigarettes? If not, what could replace them that's equally profitable? As a partial solution to this problem, big drugstore chains like Walgreens now sell cigarettes and smoking cessation products such as Nicorette and the patch right next to one another.

An additional point about drugstore and C-store markets: their sales of tobacco are geared heavily to the communities they serve. In high-end neighborhoods, cigarette sales are minimal. The denizens of these hamlets have for all intents and purposes kicked the habit. In more blue-collar communities, the number of people who smoke is much higher. Yes, everyone knows by now what cigarettes do to you. But if your financial resources are limited, smoking more than ever becomes a small source of relaxation and, despite the ever-rising prices of cigarettes, a relatively inexpensive form of self-indulgence. In a higher-end community, you could perhaps relieve that same impulse by buying a new blouse or taking a joyride in your convertible BMW. Smoking is all about punctuating time—adding commas, periods, and semicolons to the hours of your day. For many other people, it's also about taking a well-deserved break.

SIN #4: WINE, WOMEN, AND SONG

We've just made our way inside a liquor store. Constructed to look like an old barn, it even *smells* like old beer suds.

In the course of all our work in liquor stores, our studies at Envirosell have demonstrated that the most single-minded, terrierlike purchaser is a male who's brand-loyal to his Jack Daniel's. Once entering the store, he heads straight to the shelf, grabs his dark prey, pays, and promptly leaves. Of all possible store customers, male and female, he is on the actual premises the least amount of time. He doesn't think of, or even consider, buying anything else. He's just restocking his supply. He'll do this, too, whether he's in a package store or a supermarket—it doesn't matter.

The female consumer is a very different animal.

Envirosell has worked for most of the major companies in the beer and alcohol business. It's work that has taken us to every class of retail that sells alcohol, from bars to restaurants, even to tasting rooms at vineyards.

As I noted in the last chapter, throughout the liquor industry, and others, marketers use three influencers to appeal to women consumers. *Light. Bright. White.* Which in this case means white wine, light beer, and anything that's luminous, sparkly, or colorful. The sales on all those products, especially white wines, have skyrocketed over the years.

Yet when you think about it, aren't these all words that connect to classic female concerns and considerations, including cleanliness and weight control? Isn't there something irrationally more slenderizing about imbibing a white wine, or for that matter, a clear substance like gin or vodka, than their woodier-looking cousins on the shelf? Not only is white wine a cleaner, less contaminated-looking mix, it also promises a lightness that may play out in a female's head as signaling fewer calories. Red wines, often described in terms of the "fullness of their body," are thus often a female turn-off, as are traditionally dark, syrupy, or mud-colored drinks that appeal to guys and which are hard-pressed to escape the whiff of Dad and past decades. Now that I think of it, scotches and whiskies are even the *color* of antiques.

A female friend of mine has heard her women friends negotiating with themselves before they go out for the night. How many glasses of wine should they drink? How much should they eat that day in preparation? That's sad to me.

Regardless, for many females, that joyful old standby, rum and Coke, is more likely today to be rum and Diet Coke.

To take this observation a step further, for women (and the occasional man) suffering from an eating disorder, a proven connection has been made between alcohol abuse and bulimia. It's not hard to see why. The female can drink, eat all she wants, absorb the alcohol, purge the beverage and whatever food she's eaten, and, in the worst-case scenario, start the process all over again.

It isn't just white wine that female consumers go for. They also tend to linger at the cordial section and engage with the selection before them. A new banana concoction, a new coffee liqueur, a strawberry something-or-other. Liquor manufacturers have found smart ways to tempt female consumers to experiment with new brands through sampling. This is a scenario in which a smiling young person stands there with a tray packed with small glasses filled with the liquor they're trying to move. A second piece of the puzzle is that women are often buying a bottle of liquor for other women. So why don't stores look more closely at where they position the bottles?

Throughout the course of our work at the global beverage company Diageo, Envirosell also found out that the one place a consumer is likely to sample a new beverage is from a friend's glass. My guess is that females share a sip more than guys tend to do. Back in the days when the company was introducing Hennessy martinis to the world, management hired young women to show up at various popular locations bearing trays filled with HMs and ask customers if they wanted to try one. These days, it's become a trend of sorts—bars that bring in liquor brands for promotional purposes. One night it'll be Beck's beer, another night watermelon liqueur, the third night absinthe. In New York City, an entire subculture exists online that tells the young and the parched where they can go that night to drink indiscriminately for free. Many an underpaid Manhattan boozehound lurches from hotspot to hotspot in search of the latest free mix.

Where do females stand with beer?

One thing we've discovered from our research over the years is that when a man walks into a convenience store (and 60 percent of C-store customers are single males) and walks out with a six-pack of beer in a brown paper bag, he's buying for himself. When a female walks into a C-store and leaves with a twelve-pack, she's buying for a social gathering, just as she acquisitions for her family within the supermarket environment. Yet the beer industry has never bothered to position beer as the quaff of choice for the female customer, or for that matter, for any kind of social gathering that centers around a meal. The tie between drinking a Corona beer with a lime and a Corona and showing a single oily sunbather taking in the rays on a Baja beach seems to be the industry's default approach, rather than showing a group of adults gathering together for, say, an ebullient Mexican dinner. The brewing business continues to focus on beer as a male beverage because historically, that's what beer has always been. The wine industry doesn't have this same problem. Yet there are meals I wouldn't dream of eating without a beer—Chinese or Thai food, or for that matter, anything spicy.

When Envirosell was doing our first work for Brahma in Brazil, we focused on making the beer sections of supermarkets more hospitable to females. Much of our approach involved replacing the signage and packaging, usually saucy, buxom milkmaids, with images of families coming together to celebrate. Brahma saw sales shoot up. Again, the U.S. beer industry hasn't taken the time to reinforce this concept as much or as well as it could.

Miller Lite—there's that word "lite" again—was a product originally oriented toward women, given its lower caloric content. The company knew full well that female consumers would be the ones buying the brand. What happened, though, was that women proceeded to bring it home, where they found that no man would even go near the thing. Eventually Miller tweaked the advertising to "Tastes great, less filling," the implication being it not only tasted good, but the male of the family would burp less. Not sure it altogether worked.

The desire to lure the female customer has also transformed the labels certain manufacturers affix to their wine bottles. An aardvark anybody? Yet here's where I think things have gone a little off-base. In my experience, a female-friendly label doesn't mean that the manufacturer should be coloring the thing Mary Kay pink. Instead, it means asking, *What is the criteria that a female brings to picking out a wine?* It may have to do with the grape and its place of origin. It may have to do with what food the wine tastes best with. Instead of answering these core questions, wine makers have gotten all cutesy with women. In my opinion, wine labels shouldn't resemble art projects. My advice is to start with a great-tasting bottle of wine, think about informing the interested shopper, *then* make it pretty.

10

THE EMPRESS'S NEW CLOTHES

I'm strolling along the second landing of this suburban Macy's department store, past kitchenware and bedding, with a detour through formal men's clothing (bathrobes, suits, camel hair overcoats, winter parkas), beside what looks like graffiti-tagger skateboarder wear for teenagers, next to a display of back-to-school lunchboxes and backpacks, which leads into the bed and bath department, which is only a stone's throw away from lamps and lighting, which morphs into electronics, which leads into, geez, how did we end up in the luggage department?

All I want is a simple V-neck sweater. Is that so difficult?

The department store is still around, anchoring one or both legs of your local shopping mall, and in some cases, serving double duty as an optional entry and exit point if the main parking lot is jammed. It's still an all-purpose shopping destination, arena, and agora, where, if she wants, a female can devote several hours to grazing through everything from belts to children's fashions to purses and handbags to chairs and recliners to patio and outdoor furniture to reading lights to Henckels knives to queen-size mattresses. In the 1860s, when the first department stores made their appearance, they gave consumers access to a spectacular array of goods and services that many had never seen before and could only aspire to. The department store was a teasing introduction to what the good life could offer—clothes, furniture, bedding, toys, and yes, cosmetics and perfume. The nineteenth-century department store was a driver of fantasy, with the only stepping-stones to attaining your dreams ambition, hard work, and upward mobility.

A nurse with smelling salts met you at the top of the escalator, just in case you were faint from the experience.

More than 150 years later, foot traffic in most department stores has slowed to a crawl. Why is this place nearly empty?

I'll answer with another question: *What contemporary female of your acquaintance has three or four hours anymore to dedicate to the act of shopping?*

As I enter the apparel section of this Macy's, I can't help but note that every inch of real estate has been divided up into discrete, well, let's call them "fiefdoms." Small branded kingdoms. Each parcel of square footage bears a famous designer's name: Ralph Lauren. Tommy Hilfiger. Calvin Klein. Liz Claiborne. Michael Kors. The contemporary American department store has migrated over to the traditional Japanese model of renting out retail space to big-name fashionistas. Consider the difference between a **DESIGNER LABEL IN BIG CAPITAL LETTERS** versus a sign reading, say, "This is where all the little black dresses are" or "Here's where you can find purses." The second option will always win. It's clear and to the point. The number of female consumers who can confidently proclaim their loyalty to Calvin Klein and their indifference to everything Tommy Hilfiger is almost nonexistent. A typical female consumer doesn't identify with a single designer. She's just looking for a dress she likes that fits her, and a purse that's calling out her name.

Just imagine if dairy, soup, or crackers were arranged similarly in a supermarket, with large poster boards overhead reading:

"Sealtest" or "Procter & Gamble" or "Pepperidge Farm." Shoppers would be tearing their hair out.

The question remains: What woman has the time and energy to stroll and cherry-pick her way through three or four floors of a department store, particularly if she's a mother toting a clunky stroller containing a baby who may wake up at any second?

Nordstrom, the fashion specialty retailer, has made some headway by rezoning the signage around women's clothing. Overhead signs spell out the style or the mood or the sensibility in question. Thus, rather than looking up and seeing "Michael Kors" or "Issey Miyake," consumers are greeted with signs such as "Classic" and "Country" and "Urban." Frankly, I still don't think females are paying that much attention.

Bear in mind that aside from its aspirational takeaways, the 1860s department store was designed for the middle-class female who came through the door with half a day to kill. Back in that era, shopping a store this size was a big deal—a treat. Maybe she'd taken a train in from the suburbs. Maybe she planned to meet up with a friend for lunch, or tea. Once there, she could eat, get her hair done, and spend what remained of her afternoon shopping or just looking around. Those were the days.

Today, while cable TV, movies, magazines, and the Internet haven't exactly taken the place of the department store, they've provided alternate venues to showcase the latest styles and fashions.

No wonder the specialty store, whether it's Abercrombie & Fitch or Urban Outfitters or Banana Republic, has trumped the department store. The time-squeezed contemporary female just doesn't have time to shop—and get lost in—a department store.

That's why the place is nearly empty.

Needless to say, specialty stores are smaller and more focused. You can get in and out in no time at all, and they give better dressing rooms. While the service isn't necessarily superior to that of the department store's, the staffers are usually better trained and more consistently knowledgeable. Department store employees are assigned a station as needed—bedding on Monday, jeans on

Tuesday, blenders and toasters on Wednesday. Better yet, the specialty store IDs itself at once. It lets you know bluntly, sometimes cruelly, whether you belong there or not, while the department store tries to be all things to all people and all ages, and thus tends to satisfy no one of any age.

Today the department store is both declining and consolidating. Both JCPenney and Kohl's are scaling back on their expansion plans. Macy's, which also owns Bloomingdale's, has undergone a large-scale management reorganization designed to cut operating costs and increase profitability. Saks, Nordstrom, and Neiman Marcus are all suffering during the economic downturn. As an entity, over the years the department store has been obliged to shed one department after another. Remember the days when you could walk into a Filene's and find a decent-looking bedroom rug, replace your old Monopoly set at Macy's, and your washer and dryer at Sears? So-called category killers such as Bed, Bath & Beyond and Toys "R" Us took away those and other markets. In turn Walmart has taken all these products and more and continues to sell them for less.

Just where is the twenty-first-century department store headed? In the context of the American market, it will never die, but it *will* get smaller. Not in terms of size, necessarily, but in terms of numbers. One possible solution slash evolution is the new Bloomingdale's in Soho, in New York City. I've heard it described as a department store that's gone to the gym. It's leaner, more tightly focused. It's designed to get you up and down four floors and out the door in an hour or less. They've reintroduced categories into the store, but in a spare, tactical way. Instead of forty LCD TVs and a dozen models of MP3 sound systems, the SoHo Bloomie's offers only two or three of each. The presumption is that someone in charge has made a sound editorial judgment on behalf of the consumer and that the only place you can find these models is right here, that is, while supplies last.

Just like the Soho Bloomie's, the specialty store takes away a degree of choice and decision making from the hands of the shopper. To many women (and men), this can come as a relief. Less is always more. The specialty store also has room to specialize in a particular demographic. It can target the larger plus-size female, who would otherwise find it a headache or a humiliation to hunt down something in her size. It can attire the expectant mom. It can dress up the tween, the teen, the college student, the wannabe prep, and the junior professional woman. Occasionally, the boutique store appears to have a soul, a passion, and even a mission. Best of all, whatever the store is—Banana Republic, the Limited, or Urban Outfitters—you can be in and out of the place in thirty minutes or less.

That said, it's interesting to observe a successful boutique work its magic, then fall off the bike. Chico's, the women's clothing and accessories store, is a classic example. Chico's had a long run of increasing same-store sales. One thing that made Chico's stand out was that it featured its own sizing charts—1, 2, 3, and so forth. Chico's apparel focused on the middle-age woman and its clothes were designed chicly and stylishly, but with a deliberately loose fit. For a time, Chico's was going great guns. Then almost overnight, management brought in a new design team, which started designing apparel for women who were looking for more precise dimensions. A longtime Chico's loyalist would come through the door, find that the store's new designs no longer came close to approximating her body shape, shake her head, and move on, never to come back. Once a store has taken pains to build a devoted female customer base, and that base finds the clothing there all of a sudden unsuitable or problematic, the customer is gone.

Gap had this same problem. For a long time, the chain's sweet spot was its denim jeans, which sold in extraordinary numbers to middle Americans. But in the late 1990s, the Gap decided to compete with American Eagle by embracing a younger demographic. Little leather vests and cutesy items began appearing in its store windows. Problem was, middle-age guys like me walked in, murmured, "This is no longer my store," and turned on our heels forever.

Gap also formalized a trend that's on its way out: unisex fashion. Unisex found its original footing inside the hair salon, where it was permissible for a male and a female to get their hair cut in the same salon, often side by side, by a barber or stylist who could be male or female. Unisex next migrated to the retail environment, with Gap in the forefront. Whether you were male or female, teenage or in your thirties, forties, or older, you could enter a Gap, make a beeline for the back wall stacked with jeans in all sizes and boot cuts, and try them on in one of the store's unisex dressing rooms, i.e., places lacking the designation "M" or "F" or even a stick figure on the door in pants or a flared skirt to clue you in. The jeans you were holding in your arms could fit you, your sister, or your brother. And that power display of colorful sweaters as you came into the store—were those meant for men or women? Did it matter, ultimately, if the red-and-green–striped one looked so good on you? One element of what once made Gap such a hot destination was the faintly transgressive idea that the sweater you'd just picked out looked just as good on you as it might on your significant other.

What killed unisex? The very lure of it in the first place. Men became embarrassed when they realized that the sweater they were about to buy was intended for females. Yet mostly I would give credit to the undoing of unisex to women. There was a hesitation on the part of the female in dealing with large, medium, and small sizing issues—and with dressing rooms shared by both men and women.

It was a telling moment in retail when Banana Republic decided to split up its stores via gender. Which is one reason why I suspect the chain has done so much better in recent years than Gap. Banana isn't going out of its way to be all things to all people and genders. As for Gap, while it may have managed its inventories well, over the past three years the chain's same-store sales have fallen roughly 20 percent.

Of course, the unisex spirit will endure, not in stores and malls but in the lives of young girls and women. For adolescent girls, boxer shorts and cotton pajama bottoms are still perennial favorites to sleep in and lounge in around the house. Then again, this might be a popular transitional stage, a tentative and literal trying-on of maleness, just as the first love object of many young girls might be a boy who's pretty rather than handsome. My significant other's wardrobe contains at least a few items that could be termed "male" (a white button-down cotton shirt, a navy blue suit jacket), whereas my own closet lacks any piece of clothing that might be considered even ambiguously female. Every few weeks, Sheryl will raid my undershirt drawer, whereas I leave hers alone. Women have always been much freer than men to kickbox the boundaries of their own gender. They're lucky that way.

Which leads me to a pertinent question (okay, it's one that makes me boil). The post-fifty-year-old female represents an enormous segment of the population that is making and controlling its own money. She controls the huge majority of passive income in the world today. She's comfortable in her own skin, knows what she likes and wants, and doesn't need a logo on her chest as a secondary form of ID. But as far as retailers are concerned, the fifty-plus female—can we just come right out and call her the Invisible Woman?—is snubbed, ignored, and airbrushed out of contemporary retailing. Size 4 rules the fashion world, not size 14. Why don't retailers get it? Why aren't they following the money?

A few brands have recognized the importance of the older market—New Balance, for one, the maker of exercise and running and walking shoes. Women's feet change with age. Ryka makes fitness shoes for women with a narrower heel and a wider forefoot, and the company also links up with women's initiatives like Avon's Walk for Breast Cancer (Ryka also partners up with Curves and Lady Footlocker to encourage women's fitness via discounting). Jeffrey, the upscale fashion and footware store in New York City's Meatpacking District, is one of the few retailers that stocks higher shoe sizes. Nine West may have a pair of shoes a female falls in love with, but the cut-off point is 11, so if you're a woman with feet larger or wider than that, your options are limited, which is why females (and the occasional transvestite) cluster to Jeffrey. At one point in our retail evolution, there was a chain of stores that catered to tall and big women. It was popular, too. It's gone now. All this despite my having pointed out time and again to retailers, particularly lingerie makers, that the over-forty female will spend far more money, time, and attention in a store than her younger counterparts. Why? Because she's shopping for underwear not as a fashion accessory, or as a garment designed to invite help removing by her partner, but for her own comfort.

Where do we find most of our attractive fifty-plus women? Consigned to elastic-band jeans and seasonal sweatshirts. A female I was once involved with must have owned roughly forty of these sweatshirts.

Another relevant issue is who, or what, is the middle-age female dressing up and down for? At age fifty, and depending on where she lives, the older woman has a variety of uniform needs. In the office, the working costume of most females isn't a pinstriped power suit, but an outfit that falls in between—a pair of nicely tailored pants and a well-constructed high-neck blouse, as well as something she can slip on over that blouse. The number of women who wear a dress to work has fallen off, and the consumption of stockings and hose is a fraction of what it once was. Retailers should take this into account.

So what does Zara know about women that other stores don't know? Zara is perhaps the most successful female franchise in fashion in the past fifteen years, a Spain-based fashion chain with more than six hundred stores in forty-six countries across the world. For the past decade, this privately held company has been the most successful global merchant organization on the planet. Its owners have no interest in talking to the press, and no need to communicate with the financial analysts.

Zara has scored several victories. First off, their knockoff speed—what we call "speed-to-market" within the industry—is incredible. See something on the runway in Paris on Monday, and it's in the store two weeks later. Zara sees, copies, produces, and delivers. Zara has also trained its shoppers to accept the asking price.

If you like the thing and it fits, buy it now, because it will never go on sale and probably will not be in the store next week. Many of Zara's factories are not in China or India, but are mostly within a few miles of the corporate headquarters in northern Spain. Store-to-factory-and-back is a closed circuit with no communication problems and no buyer jet lag. The store's replenishment cycle is usually days, not weeks or months. Meaning, if a size-10 green blouse is selling out, Zara is able to find it and restock it swiftly. When you think of other brands like Tommy Hilfiger or Calvin Klein, where the headquarters may be in New York, and the sourcing—that is, where the clothing is actually made—in China, or Vietnam, you can see the obvious advantages. For the fashion-forward female who aspires to look stylish, but who can't afford to buy on the department-store level, Zara (just like Mango and H&M) has been the apparel equivalent of the revolution fostered in drugstores and groceries by private, or store, label.

The private label movement is challenging the linkages between price and the customer's concept of value. No longer is the private label purchase driven by economic necessity or compromise. Consumer and women's magazines have pointed out there's often little difference in quality or taste. Trader Joe's and its parent company, Aldi, have built stores around private label that have fostered enormous customer loyalty. Buying private label is being increasingly seen as being a responsible consumer, like driving a Prius even though you can afford something smaller, faster, and pricier.

When I talk to my British friends about Zara, they turn up their noses. To hear it from them, Zara's success and dominance rests on the exploitation of the poor Spanish workforce in Bilbao and Galicia. It's a franchise that's managed to exploit the entire chain of women from one end to another. They sell—so the anti-Zara argument goes—poorly made garments they have stolen from other people's designs, which they then sell at an obscene rate of profit. At some point, karma is going to catch up with them.

On the other hand—and it's a big hand—Zara is a company comprised of 90 percent women, which is, to say the least, different from any of the other fashion companies. In New York, fashion is still a garmento business, a triumph of processing through male tailors. Traditionally, if you are a *schmatte* dealer, and Saks gives you an order, you give that order to a factory, who will give you a certain number of percentage points to the dollar, and pay you immediately. Thus, rather than having to wait ninety days, you can get paid immediately. The American fashion industry is completely dependent on the existence of factors. Zara, however, takes that fashion paradigm and turns it upside down, thanks in large part of its female workforce.

It's working, too. While apparel sales at both Walmart and Target have been declining, Zara has stepped in to offer a cheap edition of everything that appears on the fashion catwalks. Zara sells its copies at a reasonable price. It carries the brand, meaning that while the object in question may have been manufactured by Zara, it's still a Lagerfeld or what have you. As for the supply, it's inexhaustible.

Across many parts of Europe, and certainly in Brazil, many young females are still living at home at age twenty-seven or twenty-eight. They have disposable income which, instead of using on rent and utilities, they spend on consumer goods. In my own Manhattan office, of the thirty staff members with desks on the floor, almost none live at home. When Envirosell opened our offices in Milan, I met a forty-year-old female receptionist who was still living at home. She paid no rent and had all her meals provided. Everything we paid her, she spent on going out, clothing, and her car. The Japanese even have a name for these adult children still living at home: *parasaito shinguro,* or "parasitic singles." In a typical U.S. city, the just-graduated college man or woman is obliged to spend sometimes more than 50 percent of his or her salary on housing alone, which doesn't leave all that much room for indulgences, much less high-end fashion. In the United States, we oblige our children to mature, and move on, a lot faster than they do in other parts of the world.

My friend Wendy Liebmann is the CEO of WSL Strategic Retail and a global trend spotter and retail strategist whose boutique consulting firm focuses on bringing consumers to stores and buyers to brands. Her firm also puts out a monthly newsletter, *Trends from the Edge,* and ongoing shopper research under the banner of *How America Shops*™, which covers emerging shopping trends, hypotheses, and observations.

"So what are you hearing from the American female about shopping now?" I ask Wendy.

"I'd say women—and men, too—are much clearer now about what their expectations are from retailers," Wendy says. "And the retailers haven't quite gotten it yet. Consumers still want value, price, and convenience. But value today is more than price. It's about good citizenship, being part of the community, and helping people to control the little things because they can't control the big things.

"I've always said that retail is the dipstick of social change. The Green movement has gone from political to moral.

"I totally agree about retail being the dipstick. Shopping to us is such an integral part of what we do, how we entertain ourselves, where we meet our friends, what our social community is."

On the topic of females indulging in the little things, it's worth noting an impressive new prototype of manicure and pedicure shops. A typical mani-pedi shop is crowded, dimly lit, and factorylike. An immigrant woman, often wearing a face mask, sits across from the female customer, diligently scissoring and tweezing away at her extremities. From the customer's standpoint, it's hard to relax, since she's not entirely sure how hygienic the tools are. The alternative is a day spa, which requires an appointment, and typically costs twice as much.

I've had a manicure only once in my life. The proprietress cut my nails back so short it was painful. Until I dealt with the industry as a whole, I wasn't aware of how prevalent the issue of fungus is, nor how common nail infections are. Customers risk contracting athlete's foot, warts, or yeast infections if salons don't disinfect their equipment properly, though even hospital-grade disinfectants can't always eliminate bacteria, yeast, or even the hepatitis C virus. Many nail salons ignore government safety regulations, such as using an emery board or a bar of soap only once, because of cost or lack of education. Scary. Some dermatologists recommend women bring their own tools to the salon. But who wants to think about it?

MiniLuxe, a local nail and beauty lounge with two sites in the Boston area, blows me away. I hope they go national someday. Aside from the mellow atmosphere, the first thing you notice is how fastidiously clean the place is. MiniLuxe knows that "clean" doesn't always mean sterile, but that it should. After every treatment, every tool is sterilized in an autoclave, a vat of heat and steam pressure. This is what dentists and surgeons do with their equipment. The tools are then sealed in individual sterilization packs. MiniLuxe even offers a special polish for pregnant women, free of formaldehyde, toluene, or DBP, which can disrupt tissue production and metabolism. Thus, in a small room radiating clean, a female can sit back, relax, and enjoy what she came for.

11

C'MON A MY MALL

I'm standing at a Los Angeles mall known as The Grove. Within its confines are the beginnings of what the mall, largely driven by the female consumer, will someday become: a complete solution for the contemporary woman.

So what makes this mall so different? The stores before me are not all that different from those you find elsewhere. A Gap Kids is a Gap Kids, no matter which way you spin it. Sure, there are some upscale tenants, including J.Crew, Nordstrom, and Michael Kors, even a Stella McCartney boutique at Nordstrom, but in general this place looks like, well, a *mall*.

The thing is, even on the cusp of a recession, the place is *packed*. Why?

What makes The Grove fascinating, different, distinctive, alive, even revolutionary, is that it duplicates the urban experience—or rather, it duplicates an ideal urban experience where various ethnicities can mix and mingle within an entirely secure environment. In Los Angeles, remember, there's no place, really, for people to cross paths. You can honk at one another from the privacy of your cars, but that's the extent of it. Here, though, there's a mix: a fashionable Iranian family over there, a couple of hip-hoppers over there, a suburban preppie couple and their two kids over there. At the same time, the mall feels safe and protected.

Among the distinctive things The Grove offers is a lawn. There is actual grass to roll on, or sit on. A farmers' market is tucked to one side, so a shopper can pick up local fruits, vegetables, cheeses, and meats for dinner. There's even a public transportation system—you can ride a streetcar! For a seven-year-old kid, that's an exhilarating lure. Name me one kid in traffic-clogged L.A. who ever gets a chance to ride a train?

Which begs the question: *What is the contemporary female really looking for in a mall?* Answer: The twenty-first-century woman with a family is looking for a safe form of escape. One element of the pleasure she derives involves looking at other people. Ideally, a mall should have some connection to the sky, a view out or upward, so her shopping or perambulating experience isn't just inward. In a middle-class society, where both Mom and Dad typically work, we recognize that the collective times a family spends together are more valuable today than they've ever been. By visiting the mall, we form a more functional family unit, and sometimes even define ourselves by observing other family units. You might even say our identities are formed. The mall is also a place where children can be taught good lessons: *Say "thank you." Don't talk to strangers. Don't cross the street. Don't touch that display. If you break it, you have to buy it.* For mothers with very small children, it's also a destination where they can meet, and trade notes with, other women with small children. Being a first-time mother can be isolating.

Another thing I like about The Grove is that when I'm there, it doesn't necessarily translate into spending money. I can wander through the place, ride on the train, listen to the Dixieland band, eat a hot dog, and keep my wallet in my pocket 95 percent of the time. So when people ask me, as they often do, *Is the mall dead?*

my answer is always an unequivocal "*no.*" But that doesn't mean there aren't malls out there that aren't dying. What it means is that in the future, we will end up judging the success of our malls by the degree to which they are able to sustain density, and to give something back to the female who has made the effort to go there in the first place—and if you hadn't guessed it yet, 60 percent of all mall goers in the United States are women.

For today's multitasking female, the *mall* has to transform itself into the *all*. The Grove understands. When will other mall operators start getting it?

While fewer than ten new enclosed malls have been constructed in the United States over the past two years, developers have been scrambling to add to and reposition existing locations. Lest we forget, two generations of Americans came of age in the mall. It was the first place they were able to see a world they knew only from TV, the first place they spent their own money and where they came across people who weren't from their school, neighborhood, or church. The mall is part of their cultural DNA.

The difference is now in what we do when we go to the mall. The International Council of Shopping Centers bluntly tells us that people are going less often, spending less time, and visiting fewer stores and that was before the economic downturn, too. Thus, it isn't that we're not going—we are just going more selectively. Every tired multitasking person who slips into a lifestyle center trying to save time and money is just saving up to go to the mall at a later point. One problem? So many categories of stores have abandoned the mall. Consumer electronics, sporting goods, toys, stationery, and books have all left for cheaper, freestanding real estate. Most American shopping malls are stuffed to the rafters with nonessential apparel, giftware, and accessories such as cards and collectible shops or stores devoted to Tibetan stone figurines or the paintings of Thomas Kinkade. We want to go to the mall, but we don't need to. We're using the mall as a place to get out of the house, people watch, hook up with our friends, eat, recreate, and maybe even do a little shopping.

Today, developers are struggling to transform aging real estate. Most malls in North America are more than twenty years old. They were thrown up fast and most were horrifically ugly the day they opened. Adding skylights and fountains helps, but most transformations are freeing one-level parking into multilevel garages, stores, office complexes, hotels, and residential housing.

Several themes shout out, particularly for the female consumer. First, as The Grove teaches us, the modern mall needs to provide a far more comprehensive solution than it currently does. As I alluded to earlier, the mall has to evolve into a place where a woman can get a key made, a shoe repaired, a plane ticket issued, her dry cleaning picked up, and that night's dinner. In the Westfield Shopping Mall in Bondi, a suburb of Sydney, Australia, shoppers can stroll into a mall complete with a daycare center, a gym, a suite of doctors' offices, assigned parking spaces for mothers with strollers, and, adjacent to the mall itself, a cluster of apartment complexes. The mall is thus not only convenient and time-saving, it's also absorbed into the fiber of daily life, as well as being a place where a woman could conceivably show up in her bedroom slippers if she felt like it. Malls are desperately seeking density, i.e., bodies. The mall that figures out how to accommodate stores that traditionally have one door, such as a Trader Joe's or a Walgreens, and then add another door that leads out onto the mall concourse, will be ahead of every other mall out there. It's a big deal in the United States when a Target exists within a shopping mall. So why isn't there a Whole Foods in a mall? I'm not just talking about urban malls, but suburban malls in the American Northeast or Southwest. Adding food, groceries, drugs, and more makes the mall more of a center—and will keep the female consumer there longer if she's not focused on scurrying back home to hit up the supermarket, finishing writing up a report that's due on her boss's desk the next morning, and returning the books to the local library before her children need to be picked up from school.

The point is, Target, Whole Foods, and Neiman Marcus can comfortably—even happily—coexist under the same roof.

Also, a mall shouldn't try to be all things to all people, and I'm not talking about ethnicity, either. A mall targeting young families, a mall for teenagers, or as I've seen in Japan, a nostalgic mall for aging seniors, are all timely ideas. Successful malls of the twenty-first century will be run by placemakers not landlords, and The Grove, with its Dixieland band, trains, and grassy lawns, knows this. Placemakers are using progressive design and activist management to give their properties more sex appeal. They are also recognizing that there are more revenue streams available to them than just sitting back and collecting rent. It may be ad revenue from in-mall signage and television. It may be through sponsorships and event making, or it could be as simple as using a parking lot creatively to anchor a farmers' market, or as they have done in Menlyn Park, in South Africa, to put a drive-in on the roof of the garage.

Recall if you will that 60-plus percent of disposable income in North America is controlled by males and females fifty and over. Most of them need nothing. They have every shirt, tie, pair of shoes, and piece of jewelry they'll need for the rest of their lives. They need only fruit, vegetables, pasta, meat, and fish weekly and annual doses of socks and underwear—everything else falls under the category of "discretionary." The fifty-and-over crowd is generally downsizing, adjusting for empty nests and aging parents. They're deciding how they will spend the last third of their lives. The challenge is not selling to them, but *through* them, to the people they care about. How does Sony and Toys "R" Us sell PlayStation 3 or the Wii to Grandma?

The era of nuclear family domination is over. Thanks to aging, divorce, and changing attitudes toward relationships in general, the composition of an American household today varies greatly. The average household on the island of Manhattan is now less than two people. It's no irony that *Two and a Half Men* and *Sex in the City* reruns have replaced *The Waltons* and *Leave It to Beaver*.

Again, the most significant change in our culture is driven by gender evolution. With women owning homes and men in the kitchen, the challenge merchants face is who to sell what to. My advice? Sell into the trend. Thus, Rachael Ray sells a line of cookware for the female hand, George Foreman sells kitchen appliances to guys, and the beauty business sells skincare to women and men of all ages.

Today's housing costs for owners are significantly higher than they were in the 1960s and '70s. The pattern of how we spend our money has shifted, too. Rent, mortgage payments, mobile phone bills, and personal electronics like pagers, PCs, and printers have negatively impacted what we spend for food and clothing. Yet BlackBerries, iPods, and mobile phones are not just technologies, but also fashion statements.

We woke up one day to find that our bellies were too big, our houses were too big, and our cars were too big. We were overretailed and overleveraged and our economic woes served to remind us of our own bloat. As chains have expanded, the merchandise mix becomes limited to suppliers that fit into the merchant's distribution system. Walmart, Target, JCPenney, and Sears cannot afford to buy from small manufacturers. Their buyers have only so much time to fill a multitude of shelves, and the result is a blinding ocean of sameness. For the stores themselves, managing what goes where is increasingly difficult, particularly when a retail network can stretch from the Florida Keys to Spokane.

Retail has to follow housing trends. One choice for retailers has been to move into a city. New York City and Chicago have both seen positive population growth and strong real-estate values. Our cities have gotten cleaner, safer, and more expensive. Urban retailing is seeing a newfound resurgence. Manhattan got its first Home Depot a few years ago. The best-performing Best Buy in the country is on the corner of Twenty-third Street and Sixth Avenue. So why are the streets empty after five p.m. in most American cities? Because there's no housing. The key to reviving any urban core is to erect an apartment complex, then convince people to make the leap and move in. Hipsters and artists show up, retail and money follows, and after a while the original settlers move on to renovate another emptied-out downtown. New York City no longer has a headlock on culture, the reason being that to accommodate a thriving arts community you first have to have inexpensive housing. No such thing exists anymore on the island of Manhattan. Austin, Texas, has pulled it off. Santa Fe, New Mexico, has done it. The same is true for San Francisco.

The Internet's impact is not just in growing sales, but also as a direct marketing vehicle that drives customers into stores and serves as a merchandising tool that can promote and inform. In malls and cities, we have reinvented the kiosk and pushcart. From downtown Los Angeles and Grand Central Station to the Paramus Park Mall, we see small merchants selling great stuff we can't find at Target. The hot magazines are about shopping. The interest in accessorizing our homes has never been higher. We spend more on candles than we do on lightbulbs.

The Grove is what the mall will someday be like—a visual experience of being in a secure multicultural setting. It's the mall as theater, the mall as make-believe, the mall as a fantasy world. Why do so many females describe malls as "depressing"? Because they are. The same chains. The same climate. No windows to the outside and, in the end, no context. A consumer could be in Macon, Georgia, or Spokane, Washington, for all she knows. Is it any wonder she comes home feeling out of sorts?

Today, when I think of other mall innovations and evolutions, I think of things that are bubbling up in different parts of the world. Dubai has a mall named after Ibn Battuta, the Marco Polo of Islam, who's justly celebrated throughout the Islamic world as an explorer. The sections of the mall are themed around his different voyages. There's an Andalusian Court, a Persian Court, a Silk Route Court, and so on. In each, the Ibn Battuta Mall attempts to re-create the feeling of Morocco or Turkey or Spain. But there are incongruities: Within the central courtyard of the Persian wing there also sits a Starbucks.

There's also innovation closer to home. In Las Vegas, you have Fashion Show, a mall where you have a central concourse space designed with a runway and a gleaming array of lights. (In Harajuku, in Tokyo, I saw the exact same thing.) Again, in Vegas, ever visited the Venetian and glanced upward to see the fake ceilings and the phony sky? No, you don't have to love it. But you do have to experience it—it's quite fantastic being able to travel to these different places, since someone has done a very credible job of re-creating them. This points to something important: The idea of a public space intermixed with pure show, rather than the mall being a preternaturally ugly concrete box with the bare minimum on the inside. Instead, some brave new mall developers are taking the theme park concept and driving it to its logical extreme.

You know what I also like within the context of the modern mall? Decent parking symbols. Recently, on a visit to an Ito Yokado in Tokyo, I was charmed by the use of animal symbols in the bicycle parking lot. I'll take bears and wolves and giraffes over "4CC Lower Level" any day. In one Japanese shopping mall I visited, they had their own parking lot staffed by guys dressed up in black trousers, white shirts, vests, and fedoras, as if out of the Dick Tracy movie. They had taken the Japanese model of the uniform and turned it into something fashionable and hip.

Outside the mall environment in Japan, the store directories in Tokyo midtown are interactive, so rather than facing a static, hard-to-follow map, you can press buttons that alert you to where you are. In general, females find it much easier to orient their way around if they can look at a 3D map. In the Tokyo subway, a housewife has come up with a map that's a marvel of innovation. In each station is a chart showing a subway car to ride in that's targeted to your desired subway station exit. It's coded by destination. Thus, if you're getting off at the Hibya station with the intention of making your way to the Hermès store, your best bet is to ride in car number six. As you might imagine, this feature is very popular with mothers and older women.

Why, you might be wondering, does so much female-friendly retail innovation take place in other parts of the world? Why does the "mall as all" concept thrive in Australia, yet barely scratch the surface here?

The answer is that in a huge, underpopulated continent like Australia that lacks density, density—and having everything available under one roof—becomes more attractive and alluring to consumers.

If we go to Japan, bear in mind that one element driving Japanese fashion culture—and Japanese shopping malls—is that young females continue to live at home throughout their twenties and often into their early thirties. Since they have no room and board to pay, young Japanese women can spend their wages on their appearance. A second element driving Japanese fashion is a public transportation system that is safe. A Tokyo high school girl can easily commute to a hotbed of teenage fashion fifteen miles away. But in the United States, how many thirteen- or fourteen-year-old girls can leave their Westchester high school and safely and confidently take the commuter train into Manhattan's Greenwich Village? How many parents would allow it? Whereas inside the Japanese Metro system, I've seen two nine-year-old children commuting alone. In the United States, that would be considered child abuse.

Also, as I make my way into The Grove's protected car terminal, I'm reminded of the female-friendly parking lots situated all across Holland. Rather than white lines painted in sequence as we're used to in America, designers have created parking spaces more hospitable to women. They're like rectangular boxes. Perhaps because of biological imperatives, Dutch designers have found that females are more comfortable positioning themselves—and their small cars—*over* something rather than *within* two defined lines. Men, owing to their own biology (and owing also to the joy they get in aiming and hitting a mark), are more at ease navigating their vehicles in between a target.

Is this a concept that may come to our shores sometime soon? Wouldn't *that* be the beginning of a revolution?

But before the revolution gets underway, may I make a couple of more suggestions to malls everywhere? The first is to give good dressing rooms. Nearly a decade ago, I happily gave up one of my weekends to tour dressing rooms at the Garden State Plaza in Paramus, New Jersey, accompanied by the eminent *New York Times* columnist Penelope Green. In one, we found a stale French fry and a wadded-up Kleenex. In others we found stray bits of shirt cardboard and probably three dozen pins. Ouch. Ten years later, in general, dressing rooms haven't improved much.

There's one dressing room concept I like, in the Kate Spade store a block away from my office. The dressing rooms are adorned with old covers of classic Penguin paperbacks—from E. M. Forster's *A Passage to India* to Hemingway's *A Farewell to Arms.* Each cover evokes an era suggestive of the style which Kate Spade handbags symbolize. As a concept, it's charming and erudite, though my guess is only one in twenty-five customers probably get the joke. I first laid eyes on it with a store employee, who didn't get it, either, and the fact that I did probably came as a result of taking way too many senior courses in English literature at Vassar College in the early 1970s.

Having said this, in my head, I keep a checklist of what makes for an acceptable female dressing room: 1) flattering (i.e., not too bright) lighting that a female who's trying on clothes can adjust; 2) enough room so that the female can a) turn around to see herself from multiple angles, and; b) safely park a stroller, if need be; 3) above all else, a dressing room *has* to be clean.

The second suggestion? Stores of all stripes must recognize that the male of the species needs someplace to perch while his wife, significant other, sister, or daughter shops. After all, trying on and rejecting multiple items of apparel can eat up some serious time. Which is why I suggest a bench, or what I like to call a "plant chair," meaning a place outside the dressing room area where a male companion can sit, as well as something for him to do—watch, or fiddle with, whether it's leafing through a newspaper, a *Newsweek* or *Sports Illustrated,* or a cable TV show devoted to fly-fishing—which is always a good idea. The male will grow less impatient; heck, he may even zone out! Knowing that he is happy and taken care of, she will shop longer. It's all good.

Marks & Spencer in London has resolved this problem in a few of their U.K. stores by setting up a loungelike waiting area. Men feel like they've died and gone to heaven. They can lean back on plush leather couches, play videos, watch a football match on TV, munch snacks, even order a drink. Smaller shops may lack the floor space and budget available for a similarly equipped space, but if they're smart and use common sense, they'll consider other alternatives to positively influencing sales, such as the placement of a few male-targeted magazines.

And after the female has closed her sale, maybe the store could figure out some way to sell the guy the issue of *GQ* or *Outdoor Life* he's halfway done reading!

12

HIGHER GROUND

It's nine a.m., Saturday morning. I'm standing on a small, crowded rectangle of Manhattan pavement known as Abingdon Square—home to my local farmers' market. I show up here most every Saturday when I'm in town.

My market isn't big—six or seven stalls in all—but I know the farmers there, and they know me and what I like, and we always enjoy shooting the breeze. For more than a decade, I've been buying my corn, beans, and potatoes from Mary, a stocky, smiley woman who *tawks* with a thick New Jersey accent. Then there's Mrs. Yeun, who sells Asian edamame, as well as an assortment of homegrown greens. She'll not only direct me to some new exotic radish that's just come in, she'll offer advice on how to cook it, too.

It's not just my neighborhood where scenarios such as this are taking place, either. Nowadays, some of the most out-of-the-way cities and towns across the world feature their own farmers' markets. It could be anything from a couple of stalls selling lettuce and McIntosh apples to twenty or more booths offering up everything from local grass-fed beef to homemade goat cheeses to regional honeys and jams and maple syrups. In the United States, farmers' markets are squeezed in next to town libraries. They've set up shop on a quarter-acre beside a shuttered Masonic lodge, or across from the town hall. Across Japan, you'll find them in highway rest stops, or near railway stations, where farmers sell pickles, sweets, vegetables, and local seafood. Nearly five hundred farmers' markets blanket the United Kingdom, too, and in New York City, on Mondays, Wednesdays, Fridays, and Saturdays, the city's best-known market takes over some pretty prime real estate in Union Square.

From where I sit, the popularity of farmers' markets, and how they've transformed what we eat—the manufacturing of food itself, as well as what's for sale in our local supermarket—can be traced back entirely—and surreptitiously!—to the female of the species.

If you think about it, the production of food has always been a male-dominated profession. At the same time, women have been the ones responsible for gathering food, preserving it, storing it, and cooking it. The farmer of 1900 had a lot more in common with the farmer of 500 B.C. than he did with the farmer of 1950. At the turn of the twentieth century, men and women both produced food. The men spent their days out working the fields, while the women toiled away in the kitchens.

Somewhere between the middle of the twentieth century and today, the female of the species was relegated to a new role: bookkeeper of the farm subsidy system. Little by little, male farmers laid off one farmhand after another—not to mention their own children—while their wives managed small back offices, separating themselves from the actual production of food. In turn, the industrial food the farmers were producing was processed by men, packaged by men, and delivered to retail shops in a formal, industrial fashion. So females dropped out of even making things like jam, much less churning butter, helped along by the appearance of household appliances and convenience foods. For the 1958 farmer's wife, the washing machine was a small miracle, not to mention a huge time-saver. (Hand washing clothes in a creek takes a lot of time.)

By 1970, farming saw a huge wave of self-sufficient but largely amateur farmers. Today, we'd probably call them "back-to-landers." Most of them wanted to be in the actual commerce of food production. They cut down trees and chopped their own wood. They kept their own chickens. That era coincided with an extremely health-conscious, vegetarian movement when consumers wanted to buy more fresh fruits and vegetables.

In those days, every single cookbook section in every single kitchen had a battered, stained copy of *Diet for a Small Planet.* Not to mention Mollie Katzens's hand-written *The Enchanted Broccoli Forest* and its companion, *The Moosewood Cookbook.* I still have mine somewhere. They were charming. They still are.

So what about gender division in the farming landscape today? The thing is, the female farmer no longer exists, at least not in any kind of historical context. Beginning in the 1990s, family farming began to erode. The sons and daughters of traditional farmers had no interest in staying on in the family business if it meant nitrates in the water, pesticides in their lungs, and cancer for their kids—not to mention dirt-caked hands and unpredictable income. A lot of farming husbands took jobs off-farm. The whole "I want to grow up to be like my dad" concept vanished—and many farming children took jobs at Dow or Monsanto. But raising organic fruits and vegetables served as a way to bring sons and daughters back inside the fold, and to restore a sense of pride and respect to farming.

That didn't mean the women ever left. Nope—women *liked* farming. They *liked* preserving. They *liked* canning. And over time, they began infiltrating universities and continued demanding healthy food as they began caring for elderly parents and caring for their kids. Then as now, females are the traditional hearth keepers. They want good, not hormone-y, milk. They want a real peach. They don't want chemicals in their food. They don't want their daughters to start menstruating at age ten or eleven. (I know from my own work in the lingerie business that the average female breast has gone up a cup and a half from the 1950s, a statistic typically attributed to all the growth hormones we crank inside industrial chicken and beef.)

Looking at it from a nutritional standpoint, women are still the domestic partners doing the majority of grocery shopping and household chores. They're working within the family budget to find a division between organic and industrial food. Many don't trust that the Food and Drug Administration is looking out for them.

That said, the contemporary female farmer is almost a gender bender. Within modern farming, the male-female division of skills and talents has vanished. There's no longer any *physical* division of labor between the two sexes, and no differences in the skills of the female and male bodies. Once the guys did all the heavy lifting, but in today's farming landscape, both sexes can operate a piece of machinery equally well. A male may be a crackerjack on the rototiller—or with flowers and bookkeeping. The female may be the one who gets a kick out of lifting fifty pounds of melons.

The evolution of farm equipment has surely contributed to the launch of androgynous farming. There would be no grass farming today—the rearing of cattle on grass rather than grain—if it weren't for Israeli- and New Zealand–made watering and fencing technologies. These sprung up as a reaction and a response to the high fat profile of meats and were widely seen as the nutritionally superior way to raise cattle, and therefore, to feed human beings. Unlike stone walls, which obviously took a team of men hours to construct, today's farming fences are light and movable. Today, any female can physically move the paddocks and let the animals stroll to the feed. And present-day watering technology allows animals to drink their fill all day.

Nina Planck is a well-known food writer and an extremely successful farmers' market entrepreneur. In 2003, she served as the director of Greenmarket, the largest network of farmers' markets in the United States. Today, she manages a dozen producer-only farmers' markets across London, serving about 150 farmers and food producers whose annual sales come to about $6 million. She grew up in rural Virginia, the daughter of farmers.

"So Nina," I ask, "to what degree is the changing status of females responsible for the way in which we eat today? For example, if you look at the proselytizers of the natural foods movement, a vast majority of them were women."

"The answer to your first question is 'a lot,' and to your second, 'yes, I agree,'" Nina says. "I don't think this is any accident, either. Women have primary responsibility for food and nutrition in the huge majority of households. Cultural studies scholars can go on and on about this, but I see it more as a biological fact. If a female has a baby, she never really loses the primal feeling of providing food for her family. It's hardwired, even if she bottle-feeds—hey, even if her husband likes to cook! That's never going to change."

"The whole world is rushing around these days," I say. "Doesn't the idea of a farmers' market run smack up against a culture that has no time to cook, to shop, and that wants to get everything done as quickly as possible?"

"Sure," Nina says. "I mean, what do you think farmers' markets are responding to? The good news is that even though industrial food marches on, everywhere I look, all my fields are expanding. There's more demand for raw milk today than there are farmers to provide it. The same goes for grass-fed beef. I can find national brands of commercial sausage without any crap in them. And I think it's great that Whole Foods banned trans fats even before the U.S. government did. It was a fantastic example of business leading the government."

Today, no matter where you live, the farmers' market movement has significantly improved the quality of life—and within those markets, the variety of goods has expanded along with the customer mix. Consumers are discovering the pleasures and satisfactions of buying direct from the source. I'm not talking about a flea market scenario where wheelers and dealers sell you junky, bruised produce that fell off the back of the truck. Unlike street markets in Europe, where many markets are made up of traveling merchants as opposed to farmers, and regional chauvinism—*our* wine, *our* cheese—is prevalent, in most American farmers' markets, the person you're buying from is the same man or woman who harvested the vegetables, caught and smoked the fish, raised the chickens, gathered the eggs, and fermented the goat cheese. There's no middleman—just you, the grower, an exchange of money for goods, and a proffering of a paper bag in which to take all your fresh stuff home.

Which isn't to say that by eliminating the middleman, you'll be saving money; the produce at most farmers' markets is just as expensive as what's for sale at the supermarket. Still, it's a trade-off a lot of us are happy to make.

One of the things I like most about farmers' markets is how they've brought life into neighborhoods that once seemed destined for collapse. Urbanites who once grew sage or basil in window boxes off fire escapes have rediscovered the ground under their feet. City dwellers are planting herbs, fruits, and vegetables in community gardens. Immigrants are growing the regional specialties of the countries they left behind—bitter melons, cilantro, *papalo,* callaloo—for themselves and their fellow expats. In cities with declining populations, suffering real-estate markets, low-income residents, and land that no developer wants to develop, small farmers' markets are providing an alternate source of nutrition to inner-city residents. Detroit has nearly five hundred of them. Retail concepts are historically linked to housing and demographic trends. If the regional mall and the big box retailer were both the results of the suburbanization of American culture, then the rebirth of Main Street and the rejuvenation of our urban capitals demand new retail solutions. The farmers' market may well be one of them.

In the United States, there's even a coupon program in place for low-income mothers with infants and children; it's paid for by the 2008 Farm Bill. The idea is to encourage women to shop for produce at farmers' markets and support farmers at the same time.

Depending on where she lives, a mother is given coupons worth about twenty-four dollars per season. She can use food stamps, as well. She attends nutrition classes, then receives a map of the farmers' markets nearest to where she lives. The WIC program—an acronym for Women, Infants, and Children—is a huge hit. Some farmers' markets are entirely coupon-based. One Latino farmer I recently heard about made $44,000 a year just in coupon sales. The WIC program targeting senior citizens is even more successful. Though they seldom have occasion to cook for others, seniors have proven to be remarkably reliable spenders once they have the money in hand.

Which comes as good news, since farmers' markets are trying to expand their reputation as a virtuous locale for overly educated white women—an outdoorsy, pretend-food bazaar for liberal, affluent consumers. One important step in diversifying the market is to bring in vendors who look like the customers the market hopes to attract. In a Hispanic area, having a market manager who speaks Spanish goes a long way.

No matter what your income or background is, farmers' markets have the ability to satisfy both the consumer and the farmer. Urbanites can reconnect to a world that isn't paved or people-clogged. In an industrialized, plasticized world, farmers' markets represent a return to simplicity and integrity.

Even the Amish have joined the organic farming movement. The traditional Amish homestead has always been set up as a family farm, with the wives as the hearth keepers. Today, naturally, they're still using tools from the early-nineteenth century, and they've never been a member of any governmental organization. But Horizon Dairy, Organic Valley, and HP Hood have brought the Amish in, and along the way, they've become certified—so today, you can find small Amish family farms run as they were back in the nineteenth century, except now they have fax machines.

While big, well-established farmers' markets attract most of the press, what I find most promising is the growth and good health of our small neighborhood markets. Farmers' markets no longer comprise a bunch of old tie-dyed hippies selling bruised turnips. The edges are remarkable. They're selling everything from cosmetics and hair products to organic clothing. With our aging population base, the phenomenon of a market coming to us, rather than the other way around, isn't merely attractive and smart from a business standpoint, it brings a sense of purpose to our public spaces, along the way igniting a nice sense of fellowship and belonging.

So how long will it be before the E-commerce industry begins re-engineering itself? As far as I'm concerned, what's missing at the farmers' market is the cybertruck at the rear of a row of stalls—a system whereby I can preorder what I like week in and week out, and at the end of my consumer experience, announce that I'm Paco GHS893, pick up my bags, and head home.

Having said this, other parts of the world are leapfrogging the United States in terms of agricultural production and marketing. I once visited an organic industrial dairy in Brazil two and a half hours outside São Paolo. Thousands of people a month make the same trip to observe the dairy at work from the safety of a large observation deck. The place manages four thousand cows. It grows its own pastures and feed, and produces yogurt, cheese, and milk, as well as its own packaging. One rule is that the milking crews have to be a husband-and-wife team, on the assumption that they live together, eat together, share a bed, and are attuned to each other's rhythms. The only time the cattle are ever in physical proximity to human beings is when they're being milked. There's a familiarity and a calm inherent in this process that it's safe to say probably extends to the cow.

Also? The Brazilian dairy uses the same water in three different ways. First, to slake the thirst of the cows. Second, to wash off their coats. Third, to rinse the milking platforms. This very same water then makes its way to a recycling center, where the process begins all over again. Visitors are given lectures on nutrition and why they should be drinking pasteurized versus ultrapasteurized milk. They're given free samples, too.

Then comes a truly magical moment. By this point, visitors have observed the animals. They've watched them being milked. They've tasted the farm's produce. They've seen how the dairy water is used, reused twice more, then recycled. They now have a core understanding of dairy and nutrition. At which point, the dairy rep says, "You've now been on the farm for three hours. What have you *not* seen here? What's missing?"

No one gets it at first. The rep rephrases the questions: "Have you noticed you haven't seen a single fly? That's because we're in a constant process of cleaning. Which is why our products cost more."

If you think about a traditional barnyard, it's filth and flies, mud and feces. But this Brazilian dairy has carried off a revolutionary feat. Visitors have now made an up-close-and-personal connection with the dairy, and the brand. As they're trucked back to where they live, most are completely sold. A 15 percent premium over and above another dairy's produce? It's worth it. The selling job had nothing to do with TV or a media blitz. It involved showing consumers the *reason* for the price differential. It was one of the most amazing marketing exercises I've seen in my life.

The thing is, whenever I bring up this concept with my U.S. clients, their general reaction is, "Boy, is that ever weird."

Don't they understand that women would go for it in droves?

If the small-scale production and processing of food has historically been a female art form, my guess is that it's partly rooted in the female love of gardening. My friend Janie Marr Werum, an organic food inspector based in Columbus, Ohio, tells me that for her, and for many females she knows, there's a spiritual element to gardening. "With today's busy lives, there's a need to dig into the soil and get that feeling of natural rhythms. In spring your flowers bloom. In December, everything is asleep, and you're in your house, reading a book. In January, you buy some seeds. By February, you say, 'Yes, spring is coming!' And the time came when I found myself less interested in watching the latest *Seinfeld* rerun and a lot more interested in natural rhythms."

Growing up, I had many encounters with females who loved to garden, to sink their hands deep into the soil. My mother took *ichibana* classes, and even hired a teacher who came over to our house to instruct her in the art of flower arranging. Even my father (briefly) showed an interest in gardening. Once, after reading a magazine article, he decided he'd grow potatoes inside shredded newspaper. It took time, money, and effort, more in the end, it turned out, than he was willing to expend. A few weeks later, he'd resumed buying his potatoes at the local market.

Me? If I ever decided to grow a garden, I would want to plant yellow basil or some other exotic herb I couldn't find in any local market. Or some sort of heirloom tomato or pole bean that pleased me in an aesthetic way.

I have a friend Christine, for example, who has become a part-time beekeeper. Christine is one of five children from a well-to-do New England family. She has a property in lower Westchester County, where she keeps multiple hives. This year, she persuaded a bunch of her city friends to let her install hives on their rooftops, which yielded about a hundred pounds of Manhattan honey. I introduced her to my friend Rob, the owner and proprietor of Murray's Cheese Shop, who packaged Christine's honey as a delicious-tasting antidote to local allergens. The stock sold out almost overnight.

For a time I considered installing a hive on my own back porch. Then Dreamboat reminded me that she was seriously allergic to bee stings. If stung, she'd turn purple or worse. I let the idea drop. But I still fantasize about someday producing apple brandy, the regional specialty of northern France. Just as the Bureau of Alcohol, Tobacco, Firearms, and Explosives has lowered the number of licenses they issue for consumers who want to open their own distilleries, today we're witnessing a proliferation of microbreweries and such for making brandies, vodkas, and beers. We're also seeing an enormous rise in organic foods sweeping our stores.

Without the influence of women, there probably wouldn't be a Whole Foods in the first place.

I'm a fan of Whole Foods. One thing I'll say about the company—it's fought back hard against its nickname "Whole Paycheck." Management has made an aggressive attempt to present the chain as a place that delivers solid value for your dollar. That said, in densely populated markets like New York and Chicago, there's no question you can hunt down many of the same things you can find at Whole Foods elsewhere, and more cheaply, too. The problem is, those items won't necessarily be found in one central location. Among its other attributes, Whole Foods is a supremely convenient shopping solution. Everything you could possibly need or want is there. It's the organic foodie equivalent of the "mall as all." It has also done a very good job of managing the customer experience inside the store. The overall operating culture is friendly. Every time I shop at Whole Foods, I end up interacting congenially with an employee, not the easiest of tasks in most retail environments. The visual richness of the stores is striking. And by using signage cleverly and well, and telling ministories about the produce for sale, as well as providing recipes, Whole Foods distracts shoppers from even the *idea* of price.

For consumers, Whole Foods has also become a solution, and a facilitator, to living a more balanced lifestyle. It's not just about great-tasting food; it's about maintaining a healthy body, mind, and spirit. Cooking tools hang everywhere. There are yoga mats and soulful exercise DVDs, organic soy candles, and natural-fiber socks and clothes, not to mention a varied organic cosmetic section. Magazines like *Real Simple* and *Yoga Journal* are on display at the cash registers. And because the stores are lit so beautifully, and the light isn't cold or glaring, consumers—females, especially—perceive the store as immaculately clean.

At the same time, I also recognize that one of the greatest organic initiatives in the market today was put forth in 2006 by an unlikely source: Walmart. Today, as many people are aware, Walmart is the largest single buyer of organics in the United States.

The upshot being that today, what began as a Green initiative—organic foods—is now a movement that transcends politics and political leanings. You can be a Southern Baptist conservative and still believe in eating wholesome food. For whatever has gone on in Whole Foods at one end of the economic spectrum, a similar movement has found its place at Walmart. And while Walmart as a company has its detractors, I'm a Walmart defender in that the chain is the last bulwark against downward mobility in American culture. Walmart has preserved a middle-class lifestyle for literally millions of citizens. The company's focus is a person who's living paycheck to paycheck. The core Walmart customer is a single mother struggling to raise her children. And clearly someone in Bentonville, Arkansas—Walmart headquarters—said, "We can deliver organics to our single mother raising her children, and make money at it, too."

In the late 1980s, General Mills hired Envirosell to study how consumers interacted with labels in supermarkets. We found that the more money people made and the better educated they were, the more likely they were to study a product's nutritional contents. Years later, when we ran a similar study in Mexico, we found that label reading was correlated to literacy, pure and simple. Aren't they one and the same, though? No. You can have a seventh-grade education and still read a nutritional label. I credit the explosion in women's media over the last decade, where much of the editorial content focuses on food. This has helped all of us wise up about what we put into our mouths.

As I walk through a large suburban supermarket two miles away from Whole Foods and Walmart, it's worth noting how organics have penetrated the middle ground, too. Two out of the fourteen aisles are devoted exclusively to organic produce—Tom's of Maine toothpaste, Annie's pasta, Pirate's Booty snacks. A rustic basket of organic apples and pears has already met me at the door, next to a selection of organic lettuce, tomatoes, and corn. The overall vibe is "local farmstand."

Sure, the organic stuff is slightly more expensive than the sinisterly perfect and sprinkler-moistened produce ten yards away, but the market is obviously responding to a movement ignited by farmers' markets and, by association, females—the desire to eat unsullied food, to invest locally in our farmers, and to feel as if we consumers have a personal stake in our cities and towns. In its way, the market is saying (after clearing its throat a few times), "We're good citizens, too!" It wasn't like this five, ten years ago. Sure, this local supermarket might be competing on one end with Whole Foods and with Walmart on the other, but there's something bigger—and decidedly female—in the air, too.

It might be the whiff of virtue.

13

DRUGSTORES

What looks like an old-fashioned country store, but isn't?

Here's a hint: Before me, in no particular order, are school binders, pens, pencils, manila folders, and computer paper. Also pool toys, sidewalk chalk, soccer balls, and Hula-hoops. Plus dark glasses, flip-flops, water guns, water wings, diving masks, thermoses, ice chests, boxes of laundry detergent, shower curtains, pet food, bags of charcoal, tins of lighter fluid, tiki torches, picnic plates, clocks, picture frames, headphones, sandwich makers, window fans, air conditioners, air fresheners, humidifiers, vaporizers, Magic Markers, the latest trashy magazines, even an aisle devoted to home offices—rolling chairs, office lamps, and such.

It's as if a hardware store were married to a supermarket, a well-lit convenience store, a Staples, a mini-Target, and a health-food emporium—all anchored by a fully staffed pharmacy.

Give up? I'm inside the modern-day chain drugstore. And it's come a long way from the little shop around the corner—you know, the one with the trim, whiskered, elderly gent behind the counter who glanced up at you over his bifocals.

Let's look around and see how this place has adjusted itself to women, who make up more than 60 percent of a drugstore's customer base. While the industry as a whole has historically been considered gender neutral, the drugstore's primary customer is a female over the age of forty. Today, more than ever, the store is organized around her needs, interests, responsibilities, impulses, and indulgences.

Like every business we've been looking at in this book, the pharmacy-drugstore industry has always been owned and operated by men. Years ago, I remember going to my first large-scale drugstore convention. Outside of a *Star Trek* convention, it was one of the nerdiest collection of guys you'd ever see. Until very recently, senior management in the drugstore industry consisted almost exclusively of male pharmacists who had moved their way up the corporate ladder.

Forty years later, things have changed. The pharmacy-drugstore of the new millennium is a fascinating work in progress, an ongoing experiment of sorts. Having recognized its customer base—female heads of households, single moms, married mothers with children—the industry can't help but wonder aloud, "What else can we sell to these women?"

When you think about it, the average female already feels comfortable and at home in a drugstore. It's where she buys her haircare products, random odds and ends for her husband and children, plus the occasional lipstick on the way out. No wonder the drugstore industry is asking, "What are other stores dropping the ball on?" Also driving drugstore produce is a pharmaceutical industry that's in flux. Historically, prescription drug purchases generated 65 percent of all drugstore profits. Today, thanks to generic drugs, competition from supermarkets and superstores like Target and Walmart, online pharmacies and such, that figure comes to substantially less. How do they make up for all that lost income?

In response, most every drugstore in the world is exploring the edges of what it can market to women, whether it's back-to-school supplies, beanbag chairs, popcorn poppers, waffle makers, snack food, frozen food, music CDs (I'm gazing at *The Best of Earth, Wind & Fire* right now), high-end and low-end chocolate, or the latest beach reads.

And why not? After all, to take just one example, the cleaning products, detergents, phone jacks, lightbulbs, and so forth that have made up the center part of the supermarket have been losing market share by roughly 5 percent a year. What the contemporary drugstore has done is to colonize these products and more, and reposition them in a friendlier, more familiar, easier-to-access environment. Great news to a female who hasn't the time, energy, or inclination to hunt down Drano in a giant supermarket, or replace a busted coaxial cable at the local hardware store.

The contemporary drugstore, the modern-day supermarket, and the mass-market store (read Walmart and Target) are all in pursuit of the very same thing—to offer a complete solution to the shopping needs and everyday problems of the twenty-first-century woman.

Drugstores are designed around the premise of the mission-driven female as caregiver. She's here to drop off a prescription for herself or for a family member. While she's here she may be picking up soap, shampoo, or razor blades for her husband or son, conditioner and emery boards for her daughter. She may be a senior who's running low on milk, or eggs, or who wants a quick, no-fuss frozen-food meal for dinner that night.

That said, it's still the pharmacy that today drives approximately 30 percent of the traffic in drugstores.

One of the most important factors in the evolution of the drugstore experience has been that over the past ten years, almost 65 percent of pharmacists coming out of pharmaceutical college are now female. A traditionally male profession has been flipped.

The drugstore industry is dedicated to enriching the relationship between its pharmacists and their customers. In a self-medicating society, pharmacists are the only healthcare professionals Americans can consult without making an appointment or paying a fee. Unlike physicians, who may be under the sway of big pharmaceutical companies, pharmacists are perceived as lacking in self-interest. It's a hugely underappreciated, underleveraged profession, given that your neighborhood pharmacist might well be more responsible for your overall health than your own doctor—and if you knew and trusted her, you just might form an informed, valuable relationship.

I suspect that many customers are unsure of the degree of expertise that goes into becoming a licensed pharmacist. Are they medical professionals, drugstore employees, or what? Want to know about vitamins, how to treat cold sores, hazardous drug interactions, or what medicines to take on an empty or full stomach? Ask your pharmacist.

Modern drugstore designers have created nooks and crannies where you can have a confidential chat with your neighborhood pharmacist, whether it's about all the information your own doctor or nurse may have neglected to tell you about, or what isn't on the side of the package or written in print so small a mouse would have a hard time reading it. In some drugstores, there's even a sign asking other customers to stand behind a line to ensure a degree of privacy. The most progressive pharmacies have designed a place where you and your pharmacist can stand side by side—again, mimicking the Sephora model, where the relationship is collegial and collaborative, as opposed to confrontational.

For women, it's probably a comfort to interact with a female. One caregiver seeks out the help and advice of another.

But hold on a sec: What's that home cholesterol test doing here? And is that a blood glucose monitor?

The home healthcare segment is one of the fastest-growing realities of American life, particularly for those of us in the baby boom generation, given that almost everyone I know is dealing with an aging parent in one way or another. Again, the contemporary drugstore is taking pains to appeal to the female, who's traditionally on the front lines of caring for an aging parent. The home healthcare market is one of the highest profit margin segments of the contemporary drugstore.

What's a woman to do once she's dropped off her prescription and doesn't feel like roaming around the store?

Take a seat on a crappy chair and bide her time.

The pharmacy waiting area is typically among the saddest places in American retail—full of sick, cranky kids and extremely tired, stressed-out moms. In this store, there are four gray metal folding chairs and a stack of dated general-interest magazines. The floor is dirty. Installing better seating remains the easiest, most expedient way of humanizing a space. The chairs before me are as immovable as the seats in a United Airlines terminal. There is no conceivable way to cluster or focus a family who's together. Imagine a female perched here in this gunmetal-gray purgatory with a squalling infant, waiting for the medicine to treat her baby's ear infection. There's literally nothing to distract the poor child, never mind Mom. I keep asking the management of drugstores, "Why do you keep using these awful chairs? How about some rocking chairs?" (The airport in Charlotte, North Carolina, as I recall, features a row of rocking chairs. One reason management installed them was to soothe or comfort infants and small children. A Southern touch that would travel well.)

While they're at it, given that their audience is already seated, wouldn't it also make sense to replace that out-of-date *Readers' Digest* with some decent signage, or health-related literature? If doctors' offices can do this, why not pharmacy waiting areas?

What I *do* like in this store is a group of hand baskets tucked under the counter of the pharmacy. In my early days working at a huge and now-defunct chain, we consistently found there to be a direct relationship between the number of baskets in circulation in a drugstore and the size of the average purchase. Looking back, it may seem like a commonsensical observation, but at the time nobody had made it yet. In a supermarket, consumers automatically grab a basket or a rolling cart; quite simply we're trained that way. What about in a drugstore? It's rare. But why bother stocking everything from Hula-hoops to *The Best of Earth, Wind & Fire* if you don't want to encourage a little impulse shopping?

Hey, I spy some shark cartilage. *Jaws* in a bottle!

Another growth area in drugstores is the vitamin and supplement aisle. It's all about self-maintenance, i.e., consumers either augmenting, or even making an end run, around Western medicine. Not a lot of consumers trust Big Pharma or believe that the FDA is always looking out for their best interests. America is by a long shot the most overmedicated nation on earth. Ponds and aquifers from Maine to the Midwest contain traces of Prozac, codeine, and estrogen (from birth control pills). What we ingest becomes part of our environment. Scientists point to some very creepy results such as more freshwater fish being born hermaphrodites.

I see this passionate interest in vitamins and supplements in part as an extension of the traditional female-driven world of herbalism.

Typically, there's an even distribution of men and women shopping the vitamin and supplement section, but companies haven't yet figured out how to sell products targeting "wellness" to men that go beyond the traditional male concerns of boosting sexual or athletic performance. How do you market self-maintenance to men in a way that doesn't turn guys off—that makes them feel good about taking preventive or prophylactic care of themselves, or just staying healthy? It's a hard sell, given that "beauty" is an inherently feminine term. Still, as many male baby boomers age, they're beginning to develop a more nuanced understanding of what it means to be healthy and well preserved: good-bye, Marlboro Man; hello, Lance Armstrong. Yes, men *can* be hunky and healthy at the same time without blackening their lungs. Guys are typically drawn to products that are aimed exclusively at them. In this category, unisex doesn't work. Hence, the preponderance of products in this aisle with punchy, manly, ejaculatory-sounding names like Energy Shooter, Energy Shot, Ripped Fuel, and most poignant of all, Rock Star.

It's worth noting that advertisers still approach male grooming as a gateway to attaining romantic success with women. By framing products in terms of female approval, advertisers are telling men that they should maintain themselves not as a matter of personal pride, or to feel better about themselves, but to attract a female version of the wolf whistle, whereas advertising targeting women has long graduated from the demeaning insinuation that females maintain their looks and fitness based on a desire to look good for men.

(Every woman on earth knows that she wants to look good for herself, and, of course, for other females.)

Could it be that many men are embarrassed to show they care about how they look? My guess is yes. One neat solution to this problem was a men's salon I once visited in a Dubai shopping mall. The salon was called 1847, which happens to be the date commemorating the patent of the safety razor. The place was completely private—colorless and windowless. Male customers rang a buzzer and were let in. The salon offered massages, as well as nail, feet, and hair treatments. No one could see the unthinkable—that many men, God forbid, take pains with their appearance.

At 1847 they could also smoke cigars and drink scotch. Try *that* at a unisex salon.

That said, a few years ago, something shifted. Many men began to recognize that looking good *mattered.* Around that time, we saw that the male customer was ready to spend money on products that made him look and feel better. I see this as a trickle-down effect of the growing female influence in our culture. To wit, the line between the sexes has gotten increasingly blurry, whether it's within an appliance store like Best Buy, or even within the contemporary relationship or marriage. In the case of the former, it's not that females are suddenly becoming interested in specs and gigabytes and RAM. It's more that men are beginning to wonder, as women historically have, *What am I getting here?* rather than simply, *What is it?* We're observing a slew of stereotypically "female" social implications for the male animal, including, but not limited to, the increased male interest in body image, plastic surgery, and other cosmetic techniques, much less body hair removal.

Recently I came back from working for Selfridges in London. In the midst of a global meltdown that was hitting the UK particularly hard, one item, I was told, was flying off the shelves. It was the male equivalent of Spanx, better known as the Equmen's Core Precision Undershirt. Its cost? Approximately eighty-five bucks. Spanx, for those of you unfamiliar with the product, are female undergarments. They're like pantyhose with the legs lopped off. Spanx get rid of lumps, bumps, and visible panty lines and makes most females look ten pounds lighter. They're a chore to put on (I've never tried, but female acquaintances tell me so), but are evidently worth the effort.

The Equmen Core Precision Undershirt is black, tight-fitting but not asphyxiating, and makes the male wearer look lean and chiseled. I recently gave one to a fashion-focused male friend. As a six-foot-six ectomorph, he doesn't need it, but he's always happy to have a new plaything. Yes, it took a little effort to get the thing on, but once suited up, his chest felt rock solid, his waist tapered, his spine was erect, and he told me he looked and felt like Batman.

When you glance across the landscape of the contemporary drugstore, for the older woman, almost everything she wants apart from fresh fruits and vegetables is here. The drugstore has also pioneered small doses of snack food. In a world of megasupermarkets and jumbo-size Costcos and BJ's, where can a female get a single can of soup or a single serving of Cheerios? In the so-called shallow loop—so named because a customer doesn't have to navigate miles of store, or deal with long lines, but can get her stuff, then boomerang back to the cash register to pay for the few staples she needs. For singles, and especially for the elderly, having a food aisle with lots of single-serve choices is a big convenience.

The refrigerator-freezer section of this drugstore is compact and targeted. There's Ben & Jerry's ice cream, and a low-cal equivalent. There are shelves of ice-cold bottled water. There's Diet Coke, Fresca, and Sprite. There's milk and orange juice and eggs. There's Lean Cuisine and frozen pizzas.

Females have historically steered away from convenience stores. Imagine a female making her way into her local C-store. The first thing she sees, next to those keychain flashlights and that countertop stack of black baseball caps, is a huge display of beef jerky. All varieties, too—barbecue, hickory, mesquite, teriyaki, black-pepper-flavored, and so on. Is beef jerky a female thing? No, it's a greasy protein snack for men. To no one's surprise, a female coming into this establishment is liable to feel she just may not be the store's primary customer.

While we're on the subject, the C-store of old used to be home base for softcore porn. Mostly it was biker chick magazines—*Maxim, Juggs,* randy guy stuff like that, plus a *Playgirl* or two. Management stuck these rags behind the counter, so only the titles were peering out, but most female customers could still feel their presence in the store. Having said this, most of the chain-run stores have cleaned up their acts. One reason is that many C-stores and gas stations are run by conservative Muslims, who weren't eager to stock that stuff in the first place.

But back to our female shopping for lightweight snacks. Another issue the drugstore profession wrestles with is, *How do we provide the contemporary female with the snack foods that are of the quality and size that she is willing to accept?* As we all know, in the United States we have a problem with o-v-e-r-s-i-z-e-d. Yet, note that the JujyFruits on display here are individually wrapped so that rather than scarfing down the entire bag (as a man might be tempted to do), the female is presented with dosage-driven, possibly sugar-free, candy. There's an enormous difference between a convenience store where men can buy an extralarge Snickers bar, drugstore where a female can go to indulge in a sugar-free Reese's.

It isn't just in terms of self-maintenance that the drugstore excels. It's interesting, too, the way in which the drugstore has pushed the envelope in terms of its capacity to help more mature women cope with aging. How many females of my acquaintance have bought their first pair of reading glasses in a drugstore? I've lost count.

There's even a term for it: *These are my drugstore glasses.*

At last—one of the rare retail establishments where the female, from cradle to middle age and even beyond, is given her due.

14

SEE ME, TOUCH ME, FEEL ME, HEAL ME

From the beginning of time, women have taken concerted pains with their appearance. The definition of "attractive," in terms of body shape, may have morphed over time (it also differs from culture to culture), but the female focus on the face, the eyes, the lips, the skin tone, and fragrance crosses all geographical borders.

The building blocks of the earliest cosmetics? Charcoal and crushed stone of various colors, mixed with oil and beeswax. Then and now, smell is largely based on floral distillations with a few animal extracts like musk thrown in.

The prehistory of cosmetics and beauty is rooted in tribal rituals, with coming of age and marriage being the most commonplace. Beauty has historically been a female art form, traditionally handed down from mother to daughter, sister to sister, or friend to friend. It has typically involved one woman ministering to another—a laying on of hands that has no parallel in the male universe. Men can shake hands, slap each other on the back, walk arm in arm, wrestle each other, or beat each other senseless, but in general, there is no such thing as peer-to-peer ritual male grooming. Men may have a same-sex masseur or barber, but both those occasions involve payment.

Until the mid-nineteenth century, the concoction of cosmetics was a home industry, with recipes passed on from generation to generation. Even the twentieth-century giants, Estee Lauder and Helena Rubinstein, effectively began their businesses in their own kitchens. The very first channels of distribution began with one female going door-to-door, selling beauty goods to her neighbors. Oddly enough, Avon—and the tribe of enthusiasts who would eventually become known as Avon ladies—was founded in 1886 by a man who traveled door-to-door hawking books, tossing in a small vial of perfume to clinch the deal. The perfume became all the rage. The books floundered. A new company was formed.

By 1900, dozens and dozens of small, female-operated cosmetics businesses had sprouted across North America. This commission-compensated selling was a revolutionary opportunity for many women, whose net income wasn't necessarily based on hours, but on their ability to network and sell. This person-to-person, living room-to-living room business model still exists with Mary Kay, Avon, and other lesser-known brands.

At the start of the Industrial Revolution after the Civil War, many females streamed into the workplace, particularly the garment industries. Women began earning their own money and enjoying a welcome measure of independence. When organized retail and the first department stores made their appearances in the mid-nineteenth century, their arrival necessitated a more formal need to create brands, as well as to acquire, distribute, and sell goods. That's when men entered the beauty business, taking an industry out of the home and installing it in a factory. Mass production ensued.

By the 1930s, the beauty and cosmetics industry was juggling three disparate distribution methods—the door-to-door sale staffed by an army of commission-compensated females; the department store brands; and the local drug and general merchandise stores. "Mass" and "class" were the terms people used to differentiate the worlds of cosmetics and beauty, the distinction having everything to do with price.

The occasions where women used cosmetics were also blurring, thanks in large part to a booming movie industry. Carole Lombard, Jean Harlow, Claudette Colbert, Gloria Swanson, et al—if these glorious, elegant, stylish, mascara'd swans were ready for their close-ups, shouldn't every woman be? The idea of cosmetics serving as a discreet enhancement to the female face was over and out. Lipstick was no longer the province of the stage actress, or loose woman, but an everyday item embraced by the masses. As beauty permeated popular culture, many women went from making themselves up for special occasions to applying their faces daily.

Through the balance of the twentieth century, the beauty and cosmetics business continued to boom. Fueled by the magazine industry, teenage girls were introduced to cosmetics not by their mothers, but by relentless advertising and gushing commentary. Many aspects of the $13 billion-a-year beauty industry were, and still are, crass, commercial, and unyielding.

Mary Kay Ash founded her direct-sales company in Dallas, Texas. She realized that her potential female hire was a wife and mother who needed a flexible schedule and part-time hours. Along with her husband, she invested $5,000 in the start-up company. Mary Kay salespeople, known as "beauty consultants," had to purchase a preliminary "beauty showcase" kit. They were taught to host Mary Kay parties, i.e., "skincare classes," inside private homes. These beauty consultants purchased Mary Kay products at 50 percent of the price, then resold them. They received commissions on the sales earned by the salespeople they recruited. I've been in hotels where Mary Kay conventions are going on—boisterous gatherings that combine heavy female bonding, camaraderie, and the unspoken desire to win the fabled pink Cadillac that the company leases to its top earners.

Envirosell started working with the cosmetics industry in late 1980s. Our first client was Cover Girl. Since then, we have bounced back and forth from "mass" brands, sold in drugstores, grocery, and mass-merchant stores like Walmart and Target, to prestige brands sold at department stores. Shortly after we started work in the industry, one cynical executive characterized the business to me as "the triumph of hope over soap."

Let's talk about the mass channels first.

A simple, utilitarian item made the cosmetics industry in drugstores possible: the wall peg. It looks like a chalky pencil with a hook at the end. It sticks out of a wall crowded with countless identical pegs. If you pull one out and hold it in your palm, it looks borderline ridiculous—how could this simple gadget have transformed the drugstore beauty business?—yet its implications were and are radical.

Before the wall peg showed up, all cosmetics were behind a counter in boxes. A pharmacist dispensed them. You came in, asked for face powder, and were handed over a small box. A certain measure of courage was attached to this transaction. The wall peg, though, permitted self-service. Organized around brands, women could touch, examine, and sometimes even sample beauty products (in contrast to the department store, where access to the product was controlled by hard-eyed and aggressive commissioned salespeople). Most importantly, the pricing was transparent. What has historically bothered younger customers was not knowing how much the product cost until they were handed the receipt.

Thanks to the wall peg, what used to be behind the counter is now in front of you. That said, the mass-market beauty industry has always been a very ordered, segmented market. Historically, three brands have "owned" discrete parts of the female face. Revlon owns color, meaning lips and nails. Maybelline owns the eyes. Cover Girl owns the face. Skincare, or what the industry also calls "hygiene products," was almost a separate category. The default face products for women were staples costing no more than five bucks. More about this later.

The self-service model within the mass cosmetic section is full of complications. Most store managers hate the section. It eats up labor cost, can be a headache in terms of shoplifting, and is difficult to keep clean. (Over the years, we've accumulated countless hours of video footage of teenage girls doing themselves up in the drugstore section—we're talking forty-five minutes of applying, primping, and posing—before simply walking out of the store empty-handed.) Historically, the brands that supply product for the store are very good at inventing new stuff, but slow to cull products that aren't working. The net result is a section that tends to be overcrowded and, more often than not, confusing.

Whether it's in a drugstore or a stand-alone beauty emporium, almost every beauty purchase involves some form of reverie—a consumer making the connection between the person who she is and the person who she wishes to be. The shopping process also involves a certain amount of what I call "info fueling." *Is this the right product? Am I choosing the right color? I think I bought this before, but the package looks different.* Every woman has a story about buying something in the cosmetics section and later regretting the purchase. Without any traditional tribal training or introduction, a typical female's access to the beauty category is a haphazard soup of dimly recalled magazine articles, ad-hoc conversations with friends, and unreliable interactions with salespeople.

The typically crowded drugstore aisle has also created a space problem, which has resulted in the banishment of nonselling square inches—namely, mirrors. Think about it from the drugstore's perspective. If you install too many mirrors in the cosmetics section, customers are going to be tearing open the lipstick and the mascara and trying them on to see how they look. Another trade-off is the one between product and promotion. If the choice comes down to installing a mirror and putting up a poster of a smooth-faced, lush-lipped supermodel in a crammed corridor, it's a little tough to get rid of the supermodel or celebrity spokesperson. After all, Eva Longoria, Drew Barrymore, and others are paid spectacularly well for their services.

The net result has been that the cosmetic section in mass channels—which, again, include drugstores, grocery stores, and mass merchants—is a source of ongoing frustration for both storeowners and consumers.

Which bring us to the department store or, as the industry calls it, the "prestige channel." Suddenly—*whoa*—that lipstick that cost four or five bucks at your local drugstore costs four times that, or more. Someone once explained to me that the most expensive part of a lipstick is the case it comes in, and two-thirds or more of what women pay for goes directly to marketing and profit.

The novice customer approaching the department store counter is often intimidated, and for good reason. The prices are often concealed and the salespeople can be predatory. Typically carried out in the front of the store, the department store makeover can be a pressure-cooker experience. For many young females, it feels as if they've been seated at the front booth in a swanky restaurant when they would have preferred the anonymity of the back counter. Afterwards, a woman feels almost mandated to buy something. (Walking away with a simple "thanks" takes major-league guts.) Recognizing this dynamic, all of the prestige brands have made an attempt to be more customer-friendly. Yet part of the problem is the department store itself, whose customer base continues to age. If you are young and hip, do you really want to shop for cosmetics and perfume with Mom at your side?

Enter the stand-alone beauty and cosmetics emporiums like Sephora, Aveda, and Origins and the reinvention of direct selling by QVC and the infomercial. The latter two offer women privacy and control within their own homes. For females who are sensitive about their appearances, or wary about joining the throngs at a beauty counter, QVC and the infomercial are like answered prayers. The pricing is overt and reasonable, the before-and-after stories inspiring, and the refrain of "But wait—there's more!" magicianly. Women can simply pick up the phone and dial a toll-free number. Similarly, QVC features entrepreneurial women who sell samples more or less directly to consumers, educating them along the way about how to use a specific product, how to choose the right shade for their skin tones, and offering tips and personal anecdotes.

Since many of us have lost a connection to our neighbors, siblings, and parents, TV and the Internet have stepped in to fill certain roles friends and family once played. In some cases, who else is going to show a teenage girl how to apply blush? As I mentioned earlier, outside of teen magazines, few American girls are exposed to anything amounting to a hygiene or beauty education.

Enter also the branded store, where prestige brands, like MAC and Jo Malone, run their own shows. These places, plus Sephora, Aveda, Origins, and others, have restored the art and craft of beauty to its original female-to-female roots, where education, ritual, and product are intertwined. Part self-service, part assisted sales, this everything-old-is-new-again paradigm represents a quiet, ongoing revolution in the beauty business.

Sephora is owned by LVMH, short for Moët Hennessy Louis Vuitton, a French holding company and one of the world's largest luxury goods conglomerates. The Sephora chain includes roughly 750 stores in twenty-one countries selling cosmetics and skincare products. When the flagship Sephora opened on the Champs-Élysées in the early 1990s, overnight it became a mecca for merchants from all over the world.

What Sephora has done is to reinvent the traditional salesperson-customer dynamic. By bringing the employee and the customer over onto one side of the aisle, and making the transaction collegial and problem solving rather than *Me* versus *You,* the store flipped over the traditional interaction between shopkeeper and customer. Another plus is that the consumer can see all the products and their prices in one place, and shop the ones she likes swiftly and efficiently.

What Sephora invented is known as "open sell." The pricing is transparent, the selling is friendly and collaborative, and everything's on display—prestige brands, private label, even popular trash-with-flash brands like Urban Decay and Buxom.

Sephora has taken the gravitas out of cosmetics buying. It's all about being playful and playing dress up—trying on colors and lips and eyes and faces just to see how they look on you. And Sephora employees are right out there on the floor to assist women in the play-acting process. I once asked the store manager at the Paris Sephora, "At what point do you offer help to the consumer?" She told me Sephora employees are trained to be watchful. They look at the way a customer's head is moving. Let's say the customer has found something cool or stylish. She's studying or examining it. A minute later, she's ready to take the decision-making process a step further. But she has questions or reservations. Now she glances up, or her head turns ever so slightly—and that's the point where the Sephora employee is trained to step in to offer assistance.

Sephora has also transformed the fragrance market. Even the most expensive perfumes are in the open, so women can get up-close and personal with them. The store features lists of its new and most popular items and also what's new. Contrast that to the traditional department store where each brand is sold at a separate glass counter, under lock and key, for fear of theft.

More importantly, Sephora has changed the *tenor* of the makeover. Again, compared to the department store, where in-store makeovers can feel faintly punitive, and the customers swirling around you range from teenage boys to leering shoe salesmen, Sephora is filled with other females happy and eager to undergo the same experience. *There's* where you'll find the mirrors—directly across from the makeover throne. Sephora's makeovers combine whimsy with sensible instruction. The experience isn't only about what the store employee is doing to you—she's also training you how best to apply the product yourself at home.

When Sephora made its U.S. debut, the chain championed the concept of sampling. In contrast to the drugstore, its rationale was that rather than obliging you to buy a forty-eight-dollar intensive eye treatment, the store would give you a sample to take home and try out. Then, and only then, you might return to the store to buy the pricier, full-size version. Samples are meant to help customers understand the justification behind buying a full jar of something that doesn't necessarily come cheap. Kiehl's is another beauty chain aggressive about handing out samples, and its program has worked out well.

Where does skincare fit in today's beauty stores? Over the years, we have observed the vaguely disquieting marriage of hygiene and beauty, medicine and commerce. The implications of this union are, not surprisingly, increased prices. A medically approved product can easily justify its sixty-dollar price tag. At Daslu, the upscale Brazilian department store, the link between beauty and dermatology is striking. Many products on display are dermatologically or doctor-approved. There's even a medical office on the premises, where a consumer can set up an appointment for cosmetic surgery. It's fair to say that a physician-approved commercial product will always trump the expertise of a salesperson who insists that X or Y is the right skincare product for you.

Personally, I find the whole thing kind of scary.

Sephora may have opened the gates fifteen years ago, but the transformation doesn't stop there. Let's head over to Aveda.

Whew, I feel calmer already. Historically, Aveda exclusively sold haircare products in salons, but they've expanded their category lines to include skincare and makeup. Still, Aveda sells one brand only, and that's Aveda. There's a Zen, spalike feeling inside the store. The products for sale are elegant and beautiful and there aren't too many of them. More than Sephora, the atmosphere in Aveda feels syntonic with the idea of beauty, if beauty carries with it an aura of serenity, balance, and wellness. There's no pounding music overhead. That subtle aroma in the air? Industry cynics call it "roast lamb," or the whiff of rosemary. You almost want to get out a yoga mat and stretch out on the floor.

"May I offer you some tea?" a young, smiling, female employee asks. She's come up behind me soundlessly, as if on rollers.

I'd love some tea.

I recognize what's going on—Aveda's store-training program calls it "the ritual." When I take the tea (there's not much of it, it's organic and not too hot), it gives the employee the opportunity to ask me a question and lull me into a conversation. After all, the product descriptions before me are so simple they almost beg for further explanation. A bottle of shampoo is labeled only, "For dry, brittle hair." This is no accident. Aveda employees are trained to spark a no-pressure dialogue with consumers. A brief description such as "for dry, brittle hair" can easily and naturally be followed by, "Can you tell me a little bit *about* your hair?" In my case, there's not much to say, but if I were a woman, I might next be cordially invited to take a seat. The employee would then guide me through a presentation of how Aveda shampoo works. It's an interesting balance—how much information do you place on the labels underneath the products, and to what extent do you permit the salesperson to fill in the rest?

There are even products at Aveda for men. Over the sparse but piercingly handsome men's care section are a cluster of simple, perfect stones, rather than, say, a photo of David Beckham in his skivvies. The bottles themselves have a cool zigzag pattern on them that's both stylish and suggestive of the American Southwest. They're rugged without overtly suggesting hound dogs, pickup trucks, or rattlesnakes. That is to say, they're manly but soulful, even evolved.

Aveda emphasizes the concept of healthy, natural, fresh-air-and-clean-living good looks—essentially a return to Mother Earth. Aveda is a tony, uncrowded response to the hard-edged, commercialized environment of today's department store. While both the drugstore and the department store aren't going away soon, their very rigidity has created an opportunity for Aveda and other standalone beauty stores to create an intimate retail experience. As with Sephora—and as we'll see in a moment, MAC—the in-store staff is involved with and invested in the female shopper, who never once fears she's a target, mark, or opponent.

Once again, I'm drawn back to the historic left-brained versus right-brained dichotomy. In one corner is a male, scientific approach—a precise, measured world of Botox injections, chemical treatments, tummy tucks, and face-lifts—which isn't to say there aren't plenty of female plastic surgeons out there. The male science of beauty involves chemical intervention and, it almost goes without saying, some form of physical penetration. Then there's the more "female" approach, which emphasizes all-natural products and treatments, herbal remedies, teas and salves, and the subtle but peremptory rejection of "beauty" proffered by the male, science-minded hand or tool. It's a dichotomy that closely mimics the psychological landscape, which offers on one hand the option and convenience of miracle drugs to counteract the brain's chemical imbalances, versus the old-fashioned talk cure. Ask any mental health professional, and they'll tell you the two go together.

The beauty industry has finally recognized that the right physical environment matters. Many contemporary females are looking for a complete beauty solution. They want their lipstick, their haircare, their skincare, and their cosmetics all situated under one roof. Like Sephora, Aveda is up front with its pricing, too—meaning there are no hidden prices to jump out and surprise or fluster a customer, which also saves her time.

In the back of the store, a female employee is giving a female customer a delicate hand massage using an Aveda moisturizer.

Estee Lauder was once quoted as saying, "If I can get a woman to give me her hand, she's mine." Again, beauty, wellness, and health have long consisted of females tending to their own gender—whether it's the female herbalist, the female nurse, or the female midwife. Also again, under what circumstances would a man ever willingly put forth his hand to another man for a rub? Whereas here at Aveda, as I observe that female employee massaging her customer's hand, well, how much more intimate can two strangers really get?

And Estee was right: The customer is at the cash/wrap right now, buying that very same hand moisturizer!

MAC is another brand owned by Estee Lauder, the company. What differentiates MAC from the Avedas and Sephoras of the world is that MAC sells to every conceivable skin tone beyond (and including) peaches and cream—the Asian market, the Latino market, the African-American market, the Middle Eastern market. MAC is still sold in department stores, but like many other beauty brands, it's also opened its own parallel stores. Why? Because in a stand-alone location, MAC, like Aveda, has complete control over the space and operating culture in a way it can't finagle when it has to share space inside a Saks or a Nordstrom beside Clinique, which is next to Lancôme, and so forth.

Not only does this MAC serve up a kinder, friendlier, gentler environment than any department store could offer, but the staff is less rapacious, too. Compared to the crusty staff at many department stores, these staffers are hip, young, and welcoming. MAC feels like a private, unexclusive club. You may be on the late side, but they're thrilled you decided to come in the first place.

No one here looks remotely nerve-wracked, just blissed-out. Unlike a woman who's being made over in a department store (where an entire Little League team might pass by and stick out their tongues at her, and probably has, too), everybody here in MAC, and in Aveda and Sephora, is here for similar reasons. At these stores, a female has permission to sit down, get made up, ask questions, and interact with a consultant who isn't talking down to her. Thus, though she may be visible to other consumers, an implicit psychological privacy is built into a public experience.

What we're witnessing is a return to among the most ancient of female traditions. Think of it as door-to-door selling, but rather than the female answering the bell, the door has come to her—and is even standing close by her side.

Inside Sephora, Aveda, and MAC, the vibe is quieter, more private and intimate. A joyful, girlish exhilaration prevails. The contemporary makeover is less about making a sale than it is about forming a one-on-one relationship—and creating a dialogue—with another female. As well, we're seeing an intriguing blend between cosmetics and science—a homemade, inherently, and historically female art form combined with its male, left-brain, alpha-hydroxy-or-whatever counterpart. Just as the latest serotonin reuptake inhibitor can comfortably share space with talk therapy, so the female and male worlds of science and nature can coexist more or less peaceably.

Yet what lingers in my mind is the vision of two females helping each other out. They may not be mother and daughter, or good friends, but they *are* relating peer to peer.

What will the future environment of beauty look like?

It will be fascinatingly, marvelously unlinear—a free-for-all. The multitasking female will go here, there, and everywhere for her beauty product solutions. Today, access to beauty is no longer based on mass, class, or prestige. That stratified world is over. Women will continue to consume beauty products at every level, from Sephora to Macy's to their favorite websites. For most females, there's no inconsistency involved in buying Toast of New York lipstick at a Revlon counter at a local chain drugstore. Alternately, they can head to Aveda for their shampoo and all-natural moisturizer, experiment with different shades of foundation at MAC, pick up a mascara wand at Walmart, and buy a pricey Swiss-made skin concoction, plus a canister of Vaseline at their local supermarket.

The World Wide Web is cross-pollinating with the mobile phone, which in turn is mixing and matching with the bricks-and-mortar world—and the contemporary female can take her beauty needs public, or private, depending on her mood or location.

She can even log onto YouTube. Lauren Luke is a twenty-seven-year-old single mother and former taxi dispatcher. Over the past year, she's remade herself into a no-fuss cosmetics and makeup expert, along the way becoming a minor Internet celebrity. Her ten-minute-long YouTube videos, taped at her Newcastle, UK, home, have thus far logged more than 50 million hits, and her YouTube channel has 250,000 subscribers in seventy countries. Ms. Luke is honest, funny, cheerful, empathic, and appealingly ordinary. She teaches women how to apply makeup, lipstick, blush—the whole shebang. Her argument is that what TV and magazines tell women about beauty is distorted and that she's spent a lifetime feeling inadequate about her appearance. I'm sure many women share this sentiment. "Beauty," in fact, is one of the top five categories of video content women hunt down on the Web.

Lauren Luke isn't selling anything—at least that wasn't her original intent. Recently, though, Sephora announced plans to market the By Lauren Luke line through a retail partnership. Lauren Luke's triumph isn't just a mark of the Internet's influence, but a symbol of beauty moving away from salespeople, supermodels, and our own twisted cultural emphasis on youth, flawlessness, and size 4.

I find this not only cool, but beautiful, too.

15

ALMOST CUT MY HAIR

Before the popularization of the mirror in the seventeenth century, we human beings gazed upon ourselves in pools of still water, in polished glass or metal, and, when none of these options were available, through the eyes of others. The mirror was and is an elegantly simple, profound invention. It reflects what we look like, and how we vary from day to day. Are we handsome, pretty, or average; fat or thin or in-between; stressed out-looking or alert; mad, sad, or crazy? Poetically, the mirror is the window to our souls.

And while we're gazing at ourselves, how does our hair look?

A random, racing glance through history reveals a few tidbits about hair that range from the gross to the sublime. An eighteenth-century Russian aristocrat may have never once washed his locks during his adult life. Members of other cultures attended to their hair only to banish lice (nit combs have been found in Egyptian tombs). Contrast this with a tradition of real-life portraiture that reveals female hair as plumage, in some cases resembling a high-end wedding cake. Marie Antoinette's three-foot-high coifs, adorned with feathers, jewels, fruit, toys, and even miniature sculptures of ships, must have weighed several pounds.

Any woman will tell you that few parts of her body inspire more pride, anxiety, or simple day-to-day inspection than the hair on her head. Female hair is both a fashion statement and an undisguised extension of the self. The relationship between a contemporary female and her locks is an evolving, endlessly contradictory slideshow. While many women embrace an organic, all-natural look, just as many if not more have opted for the artifice of an unorganic, unnatural look—read: color.

Styling another woman's hair was among the first professions that allowed a female to step away from preparing food, childcare, or toiling in the fields. Centuries later, the hair salon industry is formidable. Some 250,000 salons employing nearly a million people exist in the United States alone. A salon's personnel are typically made up of entry-level haircutters all the way up to veterans. One young female acquaintance has had her hair cut at both the $130 and $500 level. For her, the expensive cut was worth every cent.

Those of us of a certain generation had mothers who went weekly or biweekly to the "beauty parlor." It was operated either by an older female or a sympathetic gay man. After undergoing a wash, a trim, and a perm, the women sat obediently beneath helmeted dryers that made them look like astronauts. Part psychiatrist's office, part consultancy, part gossip hive, part escape from domestic life, the beauty parlor visit was a mixture of therapy, self-maintenance, and community unlike any other within the female commercial world.

Today's beauty salons don't just offer traditional haircare. Many also offer nail treatments, therapeutic body treatments, tanning and massage, and hair-removal services. Quite a few also sell beauty products in a consultative manner. Paul Mitchell, for instance, will compensate a salon owner in return for a prominent and exclusive display of Paul Mitchell beauty products. In return, the company assumes the salon's stylists (rewarded with commissions) will subtly or overtly push the products, the assumption being that if stylists have your hair in their hands, surely they must know what's best.

The combination salon-day spa is among the fastest-growing segments of the modern beauty industry. In the future, it's expected to expand, as well as to incorporate education and instruction for at-home wellness maintenance. The most popular salon-spa services are pedicures and exfoliation. The reemergence of the beauty salon has come on the heels of the uneven success that's the unisex salon. Gender neutrality may be compelling at a certain age—just visit any co-ed college dormitory—but even at colleges, two co-ed bathrooms will generally morph into an ordered, segregated system, with the males using one, the females the other.

Unisex salons may still be ubiquitous, but many women I know find them disagreeable. It isn't the presence of males that's a problem, but rather the inherent suspicion that a stylist who can cut men's hair probably lacks the capacity to handle female hair with heightened finesse, detail, or expertise. The unisex salon can also feel faintly rote. I understand the sentiment, and my distaste goes one further—I dislike the smell of "cooking" hair.

A female may compromise one night on her meal selection, a brand of seltzer water, or a lipstick that's not quite what she had in mind. None of these choices have ramifications that last longer than twenty-four hours. A bad haircut lives in infamy.

For the female under thirty, hair is a style and personality issue. For the over-thirty female, the issue of getting your hair cut is a matter of maintenance, carried out every three months, six months, or whenever they feel the time is right. Women often alter their hairstyles after a romantic breakup. It's a reward, an ending, and a beginning. Many women are known to cut their hair short after becoming mothers, as if to emphasize the no-fuss practicality of nourishing new life. It's not only about her anymore. Typically, she'll later grow her hair out again. Still, while females have far greater latitude than men to kick-box gender boundaries in everything from clothing to sports to tastes in books, music, or art, they're limited as far as their hair is concerned. I could shave off my beard tomorrow and many people wouldn't recognize me. A female friend in her eighties told me once she'd never once in her life experienced penis envy, but she did occasionally suffer from facial hair envy.

A woman's only alternative? Wigs and hair extensions, which allow her to alter the volume, texture, length, and color of her hair, even the shape of her head. Many wigs, save the jokey Halloween ones, are made from human hair. Charities exist where women can donate their shorn tresses to make wigs for women who've lost their hair to cancer. I own one myself, passed on to me by my father. It's salt-and-pepper (salt, mostly), tousled, and evokes the 'do of a shaggy, aging Southern Californian hipster. I don't wear it. I bring it out only when I want to pull a fast one on someone.

Also on the subject of one's tresses, no man I've ever met has ever told me he's having a bad hair day (BHD). Personally, I don't think I've ever had a BHD. If I did, I wasn't aware.

A bad hair day, as many women know, is a twenty-four-hour period when a female's hair is not cooperating as it's supposed to. Female hair can be unruly in various ways. It can look, feel, and act dirty, limp, unlustrous, or wayward. Weather conditions do a number, too. When it's humid, a woman's hair can get frizzy. If she's in an overheated building or a dry airplane, her hair can lose moisture. Away from home, the quality of the water, the soap, or the shampoo in a different city or hotel can turn a restful sleep into a frantic morning.

The good news is that a bad hair day, while troubling, is by its nature fleeting.

Our culture is more and more focused on the natural, the organic, and the environmentally conscientious. Youth, glorified in fashion magazines, celebrates a fresh, untouched beauty, never mind that it involves teams of stylists and in some cases a wind machine to create it. Having said this, though, approximately 60 percent of all adult American females have colored their hair in the past year. It starts as a fashion statement in their late teens when trying out colors is easy—a fun experiment. At some point in a woman's thirties, it crosses a critical divide where it goes from fashion statement to ongoing staple as a way of managing incoming gray, and/or to maintain her hair's original shade.

Once a woman begins coloring her hair, it's difficult to stop. Hair salons heavily push hair-coloring products, too. There's also an extensive at-home self-coloring industry. Coloring is only the beginning. Hair striping or highlighting is a contemporary fad, as well—"making you look like you just came home from a month at the beach." Natural hair-coloring products may share shelf space with the more "toxic" stuff, but many women bypass them, believing they won't do the job as well.

Yet the female has a far different relationship to the hair on their heads than she does with the hair elsewhere on her body. I once heard a male anchorman on a popular TV sports network joking openly about how a female sideline reporter needed to wax her arms—the implication being that if a woman hasn't attended to excess arm hair, she's let down the ideals of a nation. The image of a female with a beautiful head of hair and a denuded body has permeated our culture. Women have accepted this dichotomy with fearsome ease and, traditionally, complicity. The top of the female head—the mane—is celebrated and accepted as a natural, essential component of the female's self-adornment, along with cosmetics and skincare. Yet the elimination of body hair on a woman's arms, legs, and elsewhere is carried out in privacy, even secrecy. This hair has nothing to do with pride, just banishment.

On one hand, the hair on a woman's head is a source of pride, whereas the hair elsewhere on her body is a challenge and a source of occasional embarrassment. It's a vexing paradox. Where and when did males and females get the idea that a woman had to eliminate anywhere from 80 to 100 percent of the hair on her body?

* * *

It's fair to say that most American males have been trained to think of female body hair as unattractive. In the United States, female body hair is practically a taboo subject. Growing up, I remember hearing jokes about European girls who didn't shave their armpits or their legs. These French or Italian females were seen as being unfeminine, maybe even unclean. Tellingly, in the United States, "armpit" has been co-opted to describe a tattered or gaseous city or hamlet.

Outside of losing her breasts to cancer, few things can devastate women more than losing the hair on her head. Across the rest of her body, it's a different story. As a young man, I can remember glimpsing a famous French painting of a female with her legs spread, her pubic hair not only visible but boldly celebratory. I found the painting erotic, beautiful, and compelling. The nineteenth century witnessed the invention of the merkin—a small wig that many females were obliged to affix to their pubic area as a consequence of hair loss caused by typhus. Merkins are still used in Hollywood movies during the filming of nude scenes.

So what's our distaste with female body hair all about?

Many of today's hair salons, as I noted earlier, offer everything from complete hair services to the partial or complete removal of body hair. This includes everything from facial hair removal to arm hair removal to electrolysis to bikini waxing to the Brazilian wax, which includes the pubis and backside, leaving behind only what's politely termed a racing stripe, or runway.

Bikini waxes are short-lived—the hair starts growing back almost at once—and are often done for aesthetic or public-display reasons. A woman will undergo the physical agony of a Brazilian typically for the pleasure or visual preference of her romantic partner.

Again, I link the Brazilian wax in particular to the decoupling of sex and procreation. It's a celebration of sex as recreation, nothing more. Few female experiences are more natural, purely bodily and ultimately human than giving birth. Yet a woman who sports no hair on her body other than on her head comes across to many men as both desirable and, in contrast with males, even alien. Blame guys all you like, but it could be argued that women are partly responsible for an unfortunate idealization of the female that ends up backfiring on many.

Ultimately, in a youth-obsessed culture with an aging-resisting baby boomer population, many females fear the arrival of gray hair. I sympathize, given differing shades of gray, some of which are purer than others. Yet a generation that grew up in stark opposition to authority has a complex time accepting the years going by—in short, *becoming* authority figures themselves. I don't remember my parents, or the parents of my friends, having this problem.

What we're awaiting, ideally, is a gorgeous model with a beautiful head of gray hair, at which point gray, all of a sudden, will become the new blonde. I think we'll accept her arrival graciously and with joyous relief. In the meantime, many females are looking left and right for an excuse, or any justification, to equate gray with femininity and beauty.

Occasionally, I will glimpse a woman on the street or on a subway platform with a great head of gray hair. Often I'll approach her, tell her how spectacular it looks. Then I move away, vanish into the throngs, so she won't misinterpret my remark for anything other than what it was—a heartfelt appreciation not just of her hair, but of her ease in her own skin.

Which is precisely what I meant to convey.

16

OFF THE WALL

OMG, I joined Facebook.

My profile page looks no different from anyone else's, save for my small profile pic—gray-bearded, a little thin on the top. Beneath the photo are a few pertinent stats, including my romantic status (taken), my birthday (December 23) and my city of residence (New York). If you want, you can poke me, write on my Wall, send me a private message or a gift, or scan my photo albums, in this case, mostly shots I've taken of assorted views from hotel rooms across the United States and the world.

I avoid 95 percent of all social or career networking media, including LinkedIn and Twitter. Tweeting just seems like one more needless digital distraction in my life, though I do reserve the right someday to change my mind. I have learned to text message, and find it nicely economical. This year, though, I wanted to find out what the Facebook phenomenon was about.

For those who aren't familiar, Facebook is a hugely popular social networking site launched in 2004 by two Harvard students. It was designed so that college students could make the acquaintance of other college students. Then it went mainstream. Today, some 250 million people across the globe count themselves as Facebookers.

No one really cares how Facebook works. The proprietors faced some scrutiny on their privacy practices—the site was storing information even after users deleted their accounts, and some personal data was made available to third-party developers. Facebook has since clarified their privacy policies. Basically, though, a technology that was designed for one thing has been transformed into something that's far more vast and influential than it was ever intended to be.

Some 110 million people in the United States—that's 36 percent of the population—are regular social networkers. Facebook itself has some 78 million regular users, defined here for our purposes as people who log in at least once a month. Facebook's fastest-growing demographic? Women aged fifty-five and over—which is almost double the number of over-fifty-five men who use the site. Married women, especially, are signing up in droves. In almost every age group, Facebook is growing faster with women than it is with men. Right now, women make up 56.2 percent of Facebook's demographic, an increase from 54.3 percent just last year. A recent article in *BusinessWeek* predicted that the future of all social media will revolve around women.

I don't doubt it.

As I said before, the two greatest villains of the twentieth century are Frank Lloyd Wright and Henry Ford, and I believe Facebook is an indirect by-product of the popularization of the suburb and of the automobile. Both have created sprawling physical distances among people. As the world gets more and more de-urbanized and people spread out, we still can't escape the basic human need to reach out and connect with friends and family.

As a person who lived in a dozen different bedrooms by the time I turned twenty-five, the access that Facebook gives me to a past I have no other connection to, and no other means of reopening, is remarkable. Facebook is a way of nourishing and maintaining what I call the weak links in my life.

When I joined, my intent was to use a veil and call myself by my given name, Francis. It did not take long to change my mind. If I were going to undergo a sincere social networking experience, I would forgo anonymity and use my better-known name, Paco. Which meant risking the possibility that an Envirosell groupie might appear in my life and I'd find his or her friend request in my inbox the next morning.

I don't post much on Facebook—usually a few words about something I've seen or read. Sometimes, if I'm feeling grouchy about an upcoming travel schedule, I'll post my itinerary for the next two or three weeks. In return, I have friends posting back in six languages—French, Spanish, Serbo-Croatian, Portugese, Hebrew, and Russian.

As for the social networking part, like most people new to Facebook, there were a certain number of names and faces that have always stuck in my head. Past friends. Old girlfriends. The human psyche will always have a detective fascination with love lost, or love gone down the tubes. It can also be interesting to find out that a classmate who was small and insecure in college is still kind of a gerbil.

To me, and to many users, I suspect, Facebook is a complete form of escape. It's like watching my own personal cable television station. You might also compare it to a long-running comic strip, or one of those serial novels popular in the Victorian age. Facebook has become an integral part of many of our lives, and I have to believe its lure derives from our ongoing desire to flee, or temporarily vanish—whether it's the individual whose spouse has gone to bed writing a long e-mail to an old college classmate, the small-town teenager talking to her glitzy friend in Manhattan, or the lonely wife catching up with her best friend from elementary school who lives halfway across the globe.

Me, I am fascinated with my friends' photo albums. Every time someone brings a camera up to his her or face, then takes a photo, it implies that the moment meant something to him or her. Recognize that posting photos onto a Facebook page takes time and effort, whether you scan it first from your printer to your computer, or upload it from a camera. One of my Facebook friends takes pictures of strange, or oddly lettered signs across America. Another takes photos of the message boards outside American churches—*REPENT YET SINNERS AND BE SAVED, DID JESUS SEND CHRISTMAS CARDS?* and so forth. If you put the photos together with the other profile information, you can get a nice capsule résumé of who this person is or, in some cases, how they would like to be seen.

At the same time I also find Facebook a little melancholy, hollow, scary. Some of the people on my friends' list are people to whom I would never post a note or letter, never e-mail, never call, never take them up on their invitation to drop by the next time I'm in town. If others were actual friends, I would never use Facebook as my primary means of communication—I'd call or e-mail them. Which begs the question: Who *are* all these assorted men and women who make up your digital social network, whom you call friends?

Existential quibbles aside, Facebook has its definite advantages—particularly for women who today are at the forefront of all Web-based social media.

Once they're on Facebook, female behavior is driven by creating and fostering relationships as opposed to, say, transactions. Far more than men, women Facebookers tend to post their family photo albums, information about their children or posts about their day-to-day lives, and even their pets. Some women's Facebook pages almost remind me of those missives that used to stuff the Christmas mailbox every year—Billy caught a six-pound trout during the family vacation in Puget Sound, Marissa is loving her first year of divinity school, our house has been blessed by a new pair of Corgi puppies christened Lennon and McCartney, etc.

For new mothers, for example, Facebook offers an online

support system, where they can trade baby stories with other new mothers. People tell me having a newborn is a lonely experience. You just want another person to tell you you're doing an okay job and that you're on track. BabyCenter did a recent survey and found that 63 percent of the females being questioned said they were active in social networks, up from 11 percent in a similar study done in 2006.

Thus, Facebook can be seen both as a means of recovering your past (or a series of pasts), and of ameliorating your isolation. Whether you're an addled new parent, or a woman whose loved one is in the military, Facebook allows you to reach out to someone else who shares your affliction or situation. It's like a self-help group you can attend without ever leaving your home—almost like an extension of Al-Anon.

It's highly likely that many older females first became aware of Facebook through their own teenage children, whether they were first concerned about their children's online safety or because they just didn't understand why their adolescent daughters and sons disappeared upstairs and shut their doors. There had to be a little revulsion or a chorus of *oh-nos* when Mom decided to sign up for her own Facebook account . . . followed by Dad.

When the older generation co-opts a totem of adolescence, usually that totem becomes radioactive. Not so with Facebook. It's still an essential site for the younger set, at least until the next big thing comes along. The number of friends a high schooler can boast is a badge of teenage status. Adolescents also make digital introductions to other kids online. Thus a friend of mine with a teenage daughter who took the ferry to Martha's Vineyard this past August found herself with a premade posse of island pals, though whether they had much to say to one another face-to-face when the ferry pulled into the dock is another matter.

What about men and Facebook? Well, males over thirty, especially if they're married, aren't rushing to join social networks in the first place (with the exception of LinkedIn, which focuses on business networking), possibly because those two words—"social" and "networking"—suggest an ongoing dissatisfaction in their romantic lives, perhaps even a wandering eye. Even after realizing Facebook isn't Match.com, many still tend to keep their personal lives at arm's length. Instead, they post info about their hobbies, recent articles they read and liked, work-related topics, or a blazing Stevie Ray Vaughn solo they stumbled across on YouTube.

I read precisely one blog every morning. It's written by my friend Christine Lehner, a novelist, beekeeper, lapsed Catholic, and one of my oldest friends. It's called Sort Quench & Dump. It consists of various dry, witty, literate mullings about bees and saints and whatever else happens to strike Christine's fancy that day. Reading Christine's blog is a ritual I enjoy with my first coffee of the day.

Blogs, a contraction of "web" and "log," are the most influential social media among U.S. female Internet users—not the most popular (that honor would go to Facebook), but the most *influential.* Roughly 42 million American women use social media on a weekly basis, whether it's via networking, writing blogs, reading blogs, commenting on blogs, leaving comments on message boards, or updating their statuses.

According to one social media study, 104 million U.S. women ages eighteen to seventy-five publish at least one post weekly, and 55 percent of women on the Internet interact with blogs in some fashion. The same study found that 12 million social media users posted to blogs, while an additional 8 million published their own, a finding which can't help but signal that female blog readers are spending less time perusing traditional media outlets. My twenty-seven-year-old assistant, Angela, for example, gets her national and international news pretty much exclusively from the Internet. While women are driven to social networks for self-expression, community, and plain old fun, if they're after information, advice, or recommendations they're apt to head to their favorite blogs.

Why are there so many more female bloggers and blog readers than there are those written and read by men? My guess is for the same reason there are so many more female book readers and diary keepers than there are male readers and diarists. More than men, women seem to like to close the drapes and time travel to another world. Often, though certainly not always, they have more time to devote to books than men. If not, they're consistently more willing to create the time. I've heard a lot of men say with undisguised pride that they have no time to read—it's as though they expect you to pin a medal on them for being active, overscheduled, and more invested in *doing* rather than in reflecting, imagining, and processing. I wish these dynamos well.

Still, I'm guessing that from elementary school on, females never outgrow the capacity for focus, contemplation, and just plain sitting still that's lacking in many men. Reading, whether online or off, has always been a more traditionally female passion than a male one. It's sedentary, meditative, personal. It's passive (I mean that as a compliment), as well as one of the few acceptable forms of antisocial behavior society encourages.

A blog by its very nature is inherently thoughtful, confessional, texture-filled, and in the final analysis cleansing.

Having said that, despite their informative or secret-sharing values, blogs can also serve as venues for public flogging. I've heard of blogs where young women excoriate their former boyfriends and/or dissect their disastrous one-night stands. Most men might mention these things to a friend, but would they go so far as to post them online? A female blogger who exposes her own self-esteem issues can find herself with a ready community of readers who understand what she's writing about, and eagerly await the next entry. Often it's easier to bare your soul to a million faceless readers than it is to an audience of one.

I also remember a blog that appeared during the dot-com meltdown of the early millennium. Launched by a guy named Philip Kaplan, it was called F****dCompany.com, a take-off on the popular business magazine *Fast Company*. It chronicled faltering or failing dot-com companies, layoffs, and closures. Disgruntled or terrified employees would forward Kaplan the correspondence their bosses had sent out, which he would then post online. Some of them were riotously funny. Kaplan not only chronicled the demise of this or that Internet company, in between he detailed his failures with various females in the course of his dating life. No woman, it seemed, was willing to give him the time of day. Kaplan ended up landing a book contract. F****dCompany.com no longer exists.

Which brings me to another incentive for bloggers. With the publishing industry more and more unwilling to take risks on first-time writers, a blog, particularly a high-concept or gimmicky one, provides an untested journalist with a built-in platform of readers. *Julie & Julia* began its life as a blog. It later became a book, and last year, a movie starring Meryl Streep. It's one of many blogs to have hit the big time.

How has the world of social networking sites affected the world of shopping? I've observed it in a couple of places. First, blogging is an informal way of trading brand names. It's an informal source of buzz—an informally effective form of viral marketing that poses another threat to traditional media advertising. I have a young Facebook friend who works in a high-end fashion store in Columbus. Her sardonic postings are often brand-devotional: "A marriage is just a marriage, but Chanel slingbacks are forever."

Every social networking site a twenty-something female chooses over a newspaper or a magazine represents another Neiman Marcus or Macy's ad she'll never see, another ad-filled television show she's not watching, another radio program she's tuning out. The most influential contemporary blogs may well be transforming the economics of traditional marketing plans. Social networking sites offer a place where consumers can edit, then disseminate, a near-infinite stream of content. When you think about it, how many of us browse YouTube? More likely, we see a video when someone forwards it to us. Social networking sites thus conduct a deft end run around the traditional marketing process and, very often in the process, get everybody talking.

Among my other Facebook friends are two local shopkeepers. Every week I get an invitation to one of their in-house wine tastings. By reaching out to neighborhood residents, they've effectively created an online community for their business, one with good word-of-mouth potential. In this sense, social networking—and Twitter belongs to this category—is ultimately a great equalizer. A small mom-and-pop store on the corner can Tweet just as loudly and persistently as a Starbucks or a Whole Foods. A marketer can create a Facebook page devoted to the glories of the new MINI Cooper or an obscure new line of women's sleepwear. Both carry the same relative weight. Again, the ultimate effect of social networking sites is to allow stores, products, and writers to shortcut traditional distribution channels by bringing ideas and products to market quickly and inexpensively.

A woman named Heather Armstrong, for instance, runs a blog called Dooce. She has approximately 850,000 daily readers. Dooce, which is pronounced like "deuce," focuses on the joys and horrors of contemporary motherhood. The writing is slangy, sardonic, exasperated, and occasionally very, very funny. JCPenney, Crate & Barrel, Walgreens, and other companies all advertise on her site, which has become so successful that Heather and her husband both quit their day jobs. Recognize that sites specifically aimed at women—from so-called mommy blogs to fashion and cosmetics sites—grew by 35 percent in 2008. Apart from politics, female-friendly categories whip every other search term on the Internet. Advertisers, who recognize that women are the household decision makers, are taking serious notice. With newspaper readership and TV viewership down and marketers recognizing the power of the female as the household purchaser, could this be the start of an obvious revolution?

That would be something to go OMG about.

AUTHOR'S NOTE

In the spring of 2006 I was staying at a beachside hotel in Dubai, and attending a conference about shopping malls. Every night management left a note in my room telling me how many different nationalities had checked in that night. Over my three-day stay, the number never went below eighty. I remember vividly one distinct twenty-first century moment. I was riding down the elevator from my room on the top floor; it stopped and what I took to be a Russian family stepped into the car—a man, a woman I presumed to be his wife, and their young teenage daughter. They were headed to the beach. The man wore Speedos and a tank top. His pale belly stuck out and the sandals on his feet could not conceal long irregular toenails. His wife was more than a few pounds past wearing her bikini with dignity. That said, to her credit she was encased in a translucent top. The daughter was skinny in her swimsuit and tight T-shirt. The three of them were escaping the cold of home and were clearly and happily on their way to a sunburn. In the American Southwest, they'd be called Snowbirds.

On the floor below the elevator stopped again, and a Middle-Eastern family of the same age and composition joined our group. Their clothes and deportment could not have been more different. The man wore a well-cut suit with a thick brocade tie. His daughter wore a pantsuit with a long sleeve top and high collar.

She had the headscarf of a good Muslim girl. The mother's black silk chador covered her body from head to toe. As the two families rode the elevator down, they tried not to stare at each other. The contrast was that extreme. The elevator door opened at the ground floor and as the seven of us queued up to leave, the chador-clad mother turned to face me. Her eyes—the only part of her I could see—were elegantly made up. They looked at me boldly as if through a one-way glass mirror—no apology, no modesty. The chador floated around her as she turned to exit, and as her body moved I had the distinct impression she wore nothing underneath. She left behind a delicate trail of perfume.

I stood frozen on the elevator. I'd been cruised and handed a cross-cultural education. All is not what it seems to be.

In the midst of social evolution, our hormonal biological heritage remains. Our hunter-gatherer programming is still hardwired. In stepping away from biology, we are testing our limits. Over the past two years of effort on this book I've flippantly described the project as just an aging guy talking about girls—a dangerous statement about a volatile topic. If in reading this I've offended you at some point, please know my heart is in the right place. My thesis is that gender evolution is both the source and the solution of much of what troubles us as a species. It is scary. In a way I'm glad I'll be six feet under when it all finally shakes out.

Several chapters in the first draft of this manuscript did not make it into the final document. A chapter on art and culture will turn up elsewhere. Isn't it ironic that the arts, from architecture to cinema, are still among the least gender-integrated institutions in the world? We can count mainstream female film directors on the fingers of one hand. Look at the world's major museums: women make up less than 10 percent of their collections. I wrote another chapter on publishing and the nature of humor; both deserved more space and thought than I gave them. Still, one of the first rituals of my cyberday is tracking down Lynn Johnson's comic strip, "For Better or for Worse." I can appreciate Tina Fey and her contribution to the outcome of the 2008 presidential election, but Lynn's family-themed humor makes me deliciously uncomfortable as she catches me time and again on the wrong side of the gender fence.

I like the idea of dipsticks—threads that give us a reliable measure of where we are as a species and where we are going. Right now I'm keeping close watch on a pair. The first is the ways in which male-female friendship will evolve, namely, how we like each other and get along personally and professionally. The second is the evolution of institutions where traditional gender roles have been largely eliminated. What happens when Male Boss and Female Secretary is no longer the absolute norm?

A few words about the first, friendship, followed by some observations about a model institution, the U.S. Army.

For my father's generation and those that preceded it, gender was a cultural dividing line. While there may have been some crossover, for the most part the boundaries were hard and clear. I can't recall seeing my father ever having a heart-to-heart talk, or even a dustup, with a female who wasn't my mother or another family member. If he had female friends, they came via my mother, or they were the wives of colleagues. If he saw them, it was always in larger social settings. As a senior diplomat he was assigned a secretary who followed him from post to post. Not once did she come to dinner at our home, nor do I remember my father ever referring to her by her first name. The only incident I remember from my childhood where I was aware that the social gender wall had been breached was at a family dinner party in our home in Kuala Lumpur, Malaysia, where the eminent Chinese novelist, Han Suyin, told my mother that she had asked Francis, my father, to run away with her and he'd declined. My mother didn't see the humor in it.

I'm a member of the first generation of males with permission to have close female friends. A few go back to high school, which means that I've known some of these women for more than forty years. Hugs, laughs, feelings, sometimes a few cross words, and yet always a valuable ongoing sense of each other's histories. I've known their husbands and boyfriends. I've been a godparent to their children. The primary bond in the relationship is clear: this man, this woman, are friends. I haven't always envied the men in these women's lives, and in a few cases I've sympathized with them.

The ability to have a female friend usually brings with it a certain comfortable distance. An unreturned phone call or missed appointment is not going to be terminal. If chance separates us for weeks or even years, it's okay. We are glad to reunite and most of the time we can pick up where we left off. We support the primary relationships in each other's lives by offering interpretation and counseling.

I function in a shopping research world filled with powerful, capable females. Two-thirds of my employees are female and a majority of the partners in Envirosell's offshore offices are women. With partners and employees, I've boarded and disembarked from planes, spent late nights getting a report out, and occasionally celebrated our mutual victories. The conversations can be professional or personal, but they are always ongoing. The liberating part? The emotional baggage is circumscribed. Being honest, reliable, and understanding is what matters most. When the connection is made the interaction is real.

How is it even possible these days for a man to have a nonsexual friendship with a female, and in the course of a single generation no less?

Well, one obvious facilitator is that a whole lot of sexual curiosity has been taken off the table. We can credit birth control—and the panorama of sexual variety that birth control has allowed us to experience—for eliminating the *What If?* factor from many of these friendships. Some guys I know ended up marrying their college girlfriends while they still were in their early twenties. Somehow, don't ask me how, they've managed to function more or less contentedly within a contemporary social and cultural environment where sexual imagery and innuendo are pervasive, and where sex has not only been detached from procreation but has become synonymous with recreation—no consequences, and certainly no Pampers or colic, required.

Yes, there are times when a friendship morphs into something else, though this is very much more the exception than the rule.

It also has gone the other way, where something begins as a dating relationship, then stalls. Something isn't right. Sometimes you back off and that's it. Or you retreat, and decide that you like each other in a different way.

The point is, nothing sexual or suggestive is in the air, not even a whiff or an undertone. Physical contact beyond greetings and goodbyes is accidental. I see no problem with this—do you? It feels normal, natural, welcome, even great. I don't even think about it much, other than the times I realize how much I enjoy, appreciate, and feel blessed by the presence of women in my life. Hard to believe my father was never privy to the phenomenon of having female friends to whom he wasn't married, romantically involved with, or related by blood.

There is still a fundamental complexity where the gender fiber can get twisted and bent. Men can and do get violent. If you compare egos by gender, the male's is by far the most delicate. It is not that we strive for equality. Instead we are looking for equilibrium. How can we get more comfortable with both the male and female sides of our makeup? I mentioned earlier that in the world of clothing, almost every woman's closet has something in it that was created with a male in mind—a blue jean jacket, a sweater, sweatpants, even a pair of shoes. If you are a man, can you say the same about your closet?

If my father's generation and mine are different, so have gen y and gen x forged their own changes. In our work as market researchers we have had to add a new social cluster. Historically as humans we have moved through life as singles, as a couple, as a nuclear or extended family group or as friends—a single sex grouping. We have had to graft onto this list the tribal unit a group of boys and girls moving together. How that pack of teenagers evolves will, in my opinion, determine our social future.

I have never served in the armed forces. During the Vietnam war, I was in school and when they instituted the lottery, my number was 217. My politics may be liberal and my social nature libertarian, but like many males I've had an interest in military history. Please take what I am about to say with a grain of salt and give me the benefit of the doubt that it all leads back to the world of shopping.

The U.S. Navy is about ships. The U.S. Air Force is about airplanes and technology. The U.S. Army is about soldiers or people, and has thus been one of the great liberalizing forces in American culture. It was the first institution that was truly racially blind, and that made the first steps toward becoming gender-blind. From officers to enlisted men and women, the U.S. Army today showcases the broadest ethnic and racial landscape America offers—a significant antidote to the injustices and prejudices suffered over the years by African-Americans, from the Buffalo Soldiers to the Tuskegee Airmen. Credit President Harry Truman for signing an executive order in 1948 that eliminated racial discrimination in federal employment. Though it didn't really take effect until 1954, it's one of Harry's greatest legacies. At the very top of the Army, sure, politics and favoritism may come into play. But once you enter the Army, up to a certain rank your advancement is based on how good a job you do, with equal pay for equal work and a transparent salary structure.

If you think about the U.S. Army as one of the largest organizations in the Western world, from both the standpoint of the number of people involved and the amount of money budgeted, it took 35 years for the system to produce its first African-American CEO, Colin Powell.

What happened with race is now happening to gender. In 1972, of the 437 U.S. Army job descriptions, only 37 were open to women. By the spring of 1973, all but 35 were open. My good friend Kate Newlin, author and shopping analyst, went through Officer Candidate School during that transitional period. She remembers her service. "In the Army, we have only two objectives: Accomplish the mission. Take care of the people. In that order. It was fabulous training."

I have a friend who entered the U.S. Army at age eighteen to escape the family farm in Minnesota. The Army sent her to Nursing School and commissioned her when she graduated. When I met her, she was a Major who commanded a US Army Reserve Mobile Hospital Unit (MASH). She was an officer first and a nurse second. The doctors on her unit reported to her. (Think about how our civilian hospital experience might be transformed if nurses ruled!) She and her unit were deployed all over the world. At age thirty-eight, she was promoted to Lieutenant Colonel at her retirement ceremony after twenty years of service. At the time she was eight months pregnant with her second child. She laughed when she told me that she thought she was the first pregnant retired Lieutenant Colonel ever. She will not be the last.

Sorting out the roles of men and women in any organization is going to be difficult. The stories over the past few years of mothers and fathers having to leave their children as their units have been sent to the Middle East have plucked at our heartstrings and forced us to ask hard questions. Legend has it that the Spartans placed into the front ranks of their Army the fathers who were able to look into the eyes of their grown sons. They'd had the chance to procreate and had the joy of watching their children grow up. How might armed conflict be transformed if fighting was limited to middle-age men?

What does the U.S. Army have to do with the world of consumption and gender politics? The world's largest bureaucracy has been hard at work on the issue of gender parity. In the midst of young raging hormones, danger, and privations, a very important experiment is today more than thirty-five years old. It's gone farther than most other major institutions in America. From West Point to the battlefields of Iraq, in the U.S. Army women have excelled.

Let's look at some of the crossovers. First some stupid points—hard bodies and camouflage are no longer the strict province of young men. While fashion has always borrowed from military pageantry, the larger concept of the outdoor lifestyle is now distinctly gender-free. You can wear your sneakers to the office, then change. Traditional outdoor purveyors like L.L. Bean, Eddie Bauer, and Nike now recognize the importance of the female customer. The supply chain business that provisions and prepares people in faraway places is what makes Walmart one of the largest and most successful businesses in the world.

Most important, however, is what men and women continue to learn about one another as they find themselves in harm's way—the understanding they will bring home and apply.

Does what I've written point to a core failure on men's part? Are we at an evolutionary tipping point in our survival as a species? As we know, men generally live shorter lives than women by five or so years. They have fewer close friends. After a period of mourning, widows often thrive. Widowers tend to lose their way. A surprising number of men and women I know had fathers they remember as inadequate. A generation later, most men are still improvising on the paternal role. Psychological textbooks generally avoid a concrete definition of what it means to be a man or a father. Women are pelted left and right with definitions of what it means to be a perfect woman and mother. It's infuriating. Yet as a species, we don't expect perfection from men. We're even wary of it. From childhood on, women are rarely granted this latitude and luxury.

As a market researcher, I've been lucky enough to get a pass on some of the boy-code. My ability to notice, process, and comment on the quirks of human and shopping behavior are my bread and butter. I may be an alpha male, but my job permits me to stand at an explicitly watchful angle to my own gender.

In the course of writing this book, I talked to a lot of women about some of my observations. Their responses have been intriguing. On one hand, many cheer the ongoing progress of females in the workplace, their increasing economic power and influence.

Women also know the power they hold is historically invisible. They are used to getting little credit for raising children, running households, working hard, and serving as the glue that holds the world together. But women must also wonder: does this mean we'll end up doing even *more* than we've been doing all these years?

Speaking as a guy, I think men continue to owe women our gratitude for leading our species forward.

Thanks for reading.

BIBLIOGRAPHY/ SUGGESTED READING

Adamson, Allen P. *BrandSimple.* New York: Palgrave Macmillan, 2006.

Ashenburg, Katherine. *The Dirt on Clean.* New York: North Point Press, 2007.

Barletta, Marti. *PrimeTime Women.* New York: Kaplan Publishing, 2007.

Benson, April Lane. *I Shop, Therefore I Am.* Northvale, NJ: Jason Aronson Inc., 2000.

Bevan, Judi. *The Rise and Fall of Marks & Spencer.* London: Profile Books, 2001.

Bosshart, David. *Cheap.* London: Kogan Page Limited, 2006.

Brown, Mary, and Carol Orsborn. *Boom.* New York: AMACOM, 2006.

Colomina, Beatriz. *Sexuality & Space.* New York: Princeton Architectural Press, 1992.

Gavenas, Mary Lisa. *Color Stories.* New York: Simon & Schuster, 2002.

Mooney, Kelly P. *The Ten Demandments.* New York: McGraw-Hill, 2002.

Newline, Kate. *Passion Brands.* New York: Prometheus Books, 2009.

Popcorn, Faith. *Eveolution.* New York: Hyperion, 2001.

Roche, Daniel. *A History of Everyday Things.* Cambridge, MA: Cambridge University Press, 2000.

Rutes, Walter A., Richard H. Penner, and Lawrence Adams. *Hotel Design, Planning, and Development.* New York: W.W. Norton & Company, 2001.

Sandoval-Strausz, A. K. *Hotel: An American History.* New Haven, CT: Yale University Press, 2007.

Scranton, Philip. *Beauty and Business.* New York: Routledge, 2001.

Smith, J. Walker, and Ann Clurman. *Rocking the Ages.* New York: HarperCollins, 1997.

Stern, Remy. *But Wait . . . There's More.* New York: HarperCollins, 2009.

Thomas, Dana. *Deluxe.* New York: The Penguin Press, 2007.

ACKNOWLEDGMENTS

Edith Raymer, my paternal grandmother, entered Vassar College as a freshman in the fall of 1912. Her Canadian father was concerned that she was going to a country filled with gangsters; notwithstanding that Poughkeepsie, home of Vassar, was only ninety miles north of New York City, his parting gift to her was a pearl-handled .25 caliber Beretta automatic (007's gun). She carried it in her purse for forty years. I like to think she was a pistol even if she carried an automatic.

Edith smoked Kents, liked bourbon, voted Democratic, and loved her husband even though he was slightly to the right of Attila the Hun. I never called her "Grandmother"—she seemed much too dignified. What I remember best about her was her elevated sense of justice. She understood that what you felt sometimes conflicted with what was right. That tradeoff is what drives social progress. I thank her for making that clear to me at an early age.

While my name may be listed in the Library of Congress as the author of this volume, it was a communal effort. Peter Smith, Angela Mauro, and Sheryl Henze all worked directly on the manuscript, albeit for different reasons. Peter worked with joy and interest; Angela, with careful attention to detail and the eyes of a younger reader; Sheryl was just scared about what trouble her significant other might be getting into.

Peter and I conducted interviews with a series of gifted and accomplished women, interviews that help drive this book's content.

Wendy Liebmann and Kate Newlin are fellow retail and marketing analysts. Martha Wilson and Lowery Sims are arts administrators and distinguished curators. Martha says that it's the arts that keep her from being a serial killer. Pam Dillon and Mary Ann Wolf are businesswomen from different ends of both the country and the business spectrum. Pam is a former investment banker and CFO for a large mall developer. Mary Ann Wolf teaches agricultural economics at Cal Poly and spent years building market research models. Janie Marr Werum is an old classmate from Vassar who spent half her career as a motion picture executive and now works as an organic farm inspector. Nina Planck is a writer, farmer's market manager, and evangelist for natural foods. All of them I think of as having some kind of pixie dust, a personal and intellectual quality that has made them sparkle in my eyes.

This is my third book for Simon & Schuster. I have to thank my agents, Glen Hartley and Lynn Chu, who have managed that relationship. Alice Mayhew is my editor yet again. Her editorial colleagues are Karen Thompson and Roger Labrie. David Rosenthal has been the gentle voice of the publisher. Again, thank you.

It's been hard over the past fifteen years to sustain relationships in my home city. I travel more than 120 nights and fly some quarter million miles a year. I return home often just north of zombie status. I tend to drop in and out of people's lives. There are a few that give me permission to leave and welcome me back. Rip Hayman and Jeff Hewitt have been watching my back for forty years. I do have a female posse—Susan Towers, Erika Szychowski, Barbara Pollitt, Haesook Kim, and Christine Lehner.

I have colleagues scattered across the world. We cross paths, sometimes often and sometimes every year or two. Yet each time we meet it is as if we saw each other yesterday. The ease is just there. Martin Lindstrom, David Bosshart, Joseph Guglietti, José Luis Nueno, Kenji Ondera, Kaz Toyota, Bruce Carpenter, Terry Shook, Abdullah Sharafi, and Jean Pierre Baade are just a few of them.

My partner at Envirosell is Craig Childress. Without his minding the fort day in and day out, I would not be able to live the life I live or undertake a project like this.

INDEX